Apocalypse Next

About IEA publications

The IEA publishes scores of books, papers, blogs and more each and every year – covering a variety of stimulating and varied topics.

To that end, our publications will, in the main, be categorised under the following headings, from May 2023 onwards.

Hobart Editions
Papers or books likely to make a lasting contribution to free market debate, either on policy matters or on more academic grounds

IEA Foundations
Primers or introductions to free market concepts, ideas and thinkers

IEA Perspectives
Majoring on current policy-focused issues

IEA Briefings
Short, punchy reports on contemporary issues

IEA Special Editions
Spotlighting lecture transcripts, celebrated writers and more

Much of our work is freely available on the IEA website. To access this vast resource, just scan the QR code below – it will take you directly to the IEA's Research home page.

IEA Perspectives – Edition 1

APOCALYPSE NEXT

The Economics of Global Catastrophic Risks

STEPHEN DAVIES

Institute of
Economic Affairs

First published in Great Britain in 2024 by
The Institute of Economic Affairs
2 Lord North Street
Westminster
London SW1P 3LB
in association with London Publishing Partnership Ltd
www.londonpublishingpartnership.co.uk

The mission of the Institute of Economic Affairs is to improve understanding of the fundamental institutions of a free society by analysing and expounding the role of markets in solving economic and social problems.

A CIP catalogue record for this book is available from the British Library.

ISBN 978-0-255-36821-6

Many IEA publications are translated into languages other than English or are reprinted. Permission to translate or to reprint should be sought from the Director General at the address above.

Typeset in Kepler by T&T Productions Ltd
www.tandtproductions.com

Printed and bound by TJ Books Ltd, Padstow

CONTENTS

ABOUT THE AUTHOR

Stephen Davies is Senior Education Fellow at the Institute of Economic Affairs. From 1979 to 2009 he was Senior Lecturer in the Department of History and Economic History at Manchester Metropolitan University. He has also been a Visiting Scholar at the Social Philosophy and Policy Center at Bowling Green State University, Ohio, and a Program Officer for the Institute for Humane Studies in Arlington, Virginia. His many publications include *Empiricism and History* (Palgrave Macmillan, 2003) and *The Wealth Explosion: The Nature and Origins of Modernity* (Edward Everett Root, 2019).

TABLES

INTRODUCTION

The popular mind today is haunted by the images of apocalypse; narratives of catastrophe and post-apocalyptic survival are prominent features of popular fiction, and television has seen several successful series with those themes, such as *Walking Dead* and *Revolution*. A thriving 'prepper' subculture of people is getting ready for an anticipated collapse of civilisation. Fears and anticipations of this kind are not found only in science fiction, technothriller novels or television and film, though. In the last two decades, a galaxy of stars of science and technology, from a former President of the Royal Society Sir Martin Rees to the late Stephen Hawking, have warned of the growing chances of a disaster that could destroy civilisation all over the world or even bring about human extinction.[1] Latterly, some politicians have taken up this theme, and not all of them do so from a 'green' position. They are joined by a growing number of important figures from the world of business, such as Bill Gates (2021).

Recently, everyone has had a taste of the kind of global disaster they had previously experienced only vicariously in fictional books and television shows. The Covid-19

---

1 Apocalypse soon: the scientists preparing for the end times. *New Statesman*, 25 September 2014 (https://www.newstatesman.com/sci-tech/2014/09/apocalypse-soon-scientists-preparing-end-times).

pandemic led to a global crisis that certainly counts as a disaster, in terms of the economic impact and lives lost, and one that massively disrupted everyday life for billions of people. More significantly, it affected the patterns and workings of world civilisation in a number of destructive ways. The sobering reflection is that this could easily have been much worse – instead of thinking about how we have experienced a disaster (true though that is), we should recognise that we have dodged a bullet or had a serious warning.

All of these dangers – real and imagined – are about the same matter: global catastrophic risks (GCRs). A GCR is a possible event that will have a global impact which is utterly disastrous and long-lasting (Schneier 2015). A simple way of understanding GCR is that, as in the fictional portrayals, we are talking about a truly world-changing event. It might destroy civilisation and usher in a new, possibly permanent, dark age. Or it might dramatically reduce global human populations, maybe even to the point of human extinction. As we shall see, there are many such dangers.

The idea of such a disaster is an old one, going back to the deluge narratives of the Bible and many other mythological traditions (Carlin 2019). In the genre of science fiction, stories about such topics can be found from the early nineteenth century onwards, and it has often been a device of speculative fiction (Wagar 1982). There has also been a long tradition of authors of non-fictional jeremiads arguing that if certain trends are allowed to continue, the result will be the end of everything. The many followers of

Thomas Malthus over the last two hundred years are an example of this (although not Malthus himself, as he was not making a prophecy).

There is something novel, though, about the last two decades or so. Concerns expressed today are not tropes of fiction or arguments of the 'if this goes on' variety (although we have plenty of those still). Rather, they are well-informed concerns of a GCR happening in the foreseeable future (Bostrom and Cirkovic 2012). As we shall see, the mathematics suggest that in many cases such possible events are bound to happen sooner or later, the only question is *when*.

This partly reflects social and technological change. Developments in the media have made people more aware of disasters happening in other parts of the world, while simultaneously making it easier for ideas and concerns about possible GCRs to spread more easily. In addition, as more people move out of subsistence living and become wealthier, so they have more time to worry about other issues, including ones that might previously not have been worth worrying about.

But there are also objective reasons for increased concern, which reflect scientific investigation. First, the range of possible GCRs has increased. The reason for this is simple: previously, the main GCRs were natural phenomena of various kinds, many of them with low inherent probability. Increasingly, there is serious concern about GCRs that arise as a product of human activity. In particular, current technological developments, combined with the way the modern social and economic infrastructure has developed, raise a number of dangers. This means there are now new threats, produced by new technology and social development (Moynihan 2020).

The second reason for increased anxiety is the realisation that the mathematics of GCRs has frequently been misunderstood. In simple language, the chances of certain GCRs happening are higher than previously thought and probably increasing. Furthermore, a GCR only needs to happen once for there to be a disaster, and perhaps for human history to come to the proverbial full stop.

This point about probability should matter to everyone, not just mathematicians. Evidence is clear that the way policymakers think about risk in general and GCRs in particular is based on incorrect statistical assumptions. This was illustrated in a non-catastrophic episode, the financial crisis of 2008. Even more alarming is the evidence that institutions such as markets do not price risk correctly and so do not perform their central information gathering and signalling function. In chapter 6, we will consider the important question of why these market outcomes occur.

On a positive note, serious thought is taking place: a number of professional research organisations and think tanks now focus on studying GCR (see the list of links at the end of this work for details). Many other organisations give the topic some attention, and most think tanks and research institutes concerned with technology and environmental or climate policy list GCR as one of their main concerns. In addition, some organisations, such as Cathedral Thinking and The Long Now Foundation, are concerned with addressing various institutional problems.

More negatively, this has not yet had a wider impact on policymaking. It remains to be seen whether the experience of the Covid-19 pandemic may change this.

How should we react to these dangers? One argument is that we should ignore them, thinking that the prognosticators of possible doom are like Chicken Little, who worried that the sky was going to fall. Proponents of this argument state not only that the chances of a GCR are so low as to not be worth worrying about, but also that taking these fears seriously will waste resources and take effort and attention away from more acute and soluble problems. There are two responses to this view: first, it underestimates the actual probability of some kind of GCR happening soon, because the way probability is thought of is faulty; second, the idea that responding to the threat posed by GCRs must compete with other useful activity is incorrect.

If we do take the advice of people such as Martin Rees and Stephen Hawking seriously, however, what should we do? It is perfectly possible and, in some cases, reasonable to conclude that the risk is real but that it does not make sense to do anything about it, at least not anything that consumes resources. This is where economics comes into play because what we are talking about here is the value of resources and the costs of different uses of those resources in terms of forgone alternative uses (opportunity costs). Questions also exist about the relative costs to put right the damage caused by a GCR and the probability of a GCR occurring compared with the cost of action taken to head off or mitigate such an event. This kind of cost–benefit calculation lies at the heart of economics. Just as we need good science and probabilistic reasoning and mathematics, so we also need sound economic thinking to avoid costly mistakes.

Given that, a striking and regrettable feature of the discussion so far around GCR is how little input there has been from economists, and how much of that has been of very poor quality. There are some notable exceptions, however. The most prominent coverage has come from Richard Posner, who has written an excellent book on the public policy response to catastrophic risks (Posner 2004). We need more of this if we are to make informed decisions as to what kind of GCR, if any, we should take seriously and what actions, if any, it makes sense to then take. Much of the reasoning required is well known to students of insurance and risk management, and there is a range of tools available to help us understand the options available.

If we conclude that the possibility of a specific GCR happening is sufficiently high that it is worth taking seriously (i.e. incurring costs to prevent or mitigate), and even more if we conclude that the possibility is underestimated or increasing, what kinds of action might we consider? It might be that some actions could reduce the *chances* of that GCR happening or even head it off entirely. In other cases, it might be that the best course of action is one of mitigation, of actions that will reduce the *impact* of a global catastrophe or shorten its duration. This could be because the probability of the event occurring is so high or because, although being unlikely to happen in any given year or short-duration timespan, we can be sure it will happen sooner or later and there is no practical way of stopping it.

There may be some cases where mitigation is not feasible, but, in that event, it may be possible to take precautions to ensure that catastrophe is not total and that there is some way of ensuring the survival of humanity, or the recovery of civilisation, in the much longer term. All of these choices need input from scientists and engineers, but also historians, sociologists and, not least, economists.

The remainder of this book is organised as follows. The first chapter sets out in more detail what GCRs are and how to define them. The second examines the mathematics regarding the probability of GCRs and the question of why so much of the thinking about this is misguided. The third sets out an analytical framework for understanding the different types of GCR and explores the question of why several of these have only recently come to attention; why they are becoming more rather than less probable; and why concern about them has intensified among the scientifically informed. The fourth chapter makes up the core of the work and contains a survey of the different kinds and categories of possible GCR. The fifth chapter addresses the big question of why we should be concerned at all about GCRs, as opposed to simply ignoring them. The sixth, which is the other main part of the work, explains how to think about this economically. It also introduces two related ideas, the comparatively well-known idea of a *precautionary* principle (but modified by economic reasoning) and the less well-known but very important idea of a *proactionary* principle, again with economic reasoning brought to bear. The seventh and final chapter looks at how, if at all, we should respond to the challenge of GCRs. It starts by unwrapping 'we' to clarify who or what should be acting and in what manner. It then explores the basic principles that should underlie responses – this involves examining the apparent (to some) tension between the ideas looked at here and free-market principles and insights. It continues by looking at some of the concrete measures that can be justified in each of the particular kinds of GCR identified – justified, that is, by a combination of risk assessment and economic reasoning. The concluding chapter examines in general terms the need for institutional reforms to many market and social institutions, in order to bring about a major shift in time preferences, discount rates and investment horizons.

1 THE NATURE AND SIGNIFICANCE OF GLOBAL CATASTROPHIC RISKS

The concept of risk is a familiar one, found in economics, statistics and probability theory, and with applications in areas such as insurance, portfolio management and gambling (Beck and Kewell 2014). It is also something that all human beings everywhere deal with constantly. Despite this ubiquity, the concept is often misunderstood, partly because on examination it proves to be complex. This is true even at the level of experts, all too many of whom, as historical experience shows, either do not fully understand the idea or approach it using a faulty set of intellectual tools. A risk, simply put, is an event that may occur at some point in the future and that, if it does occur, will lead to a loss for the person bearing it. The term also refers to the chance or probability of the event coming to pass, when this can be calculated. This can be expressed in several different ways, but the usual one is as a probability in a given period of time, which can be anything from a single moment (as in the spin of a roulette wheel) to a much longer period.

It is this last that leads to many intuitive misunderstandings, which often prove costly for some but are lucrative for others. As set out here, a risk is a logically possible event that results in costs if it occurs. Not all risks (possible events) come with risks (calculable probabilities); the probability of some events happening is unknowable, in which case we are talking of uncertainty rather than risk or known probability. Incalculability, however, does not preclude making a judgement of probability.

An even more troublesome category exists, of events that might happen in the future which lead to costs but which are radically unexpected – in these cases, it is not the probability of the occurrence that is unknown but the actual event itself. You might suppose that unknowable and incalculable risks are not worth bothering about, but that is not the case.

So, two of the central components of risk are *probability* and *cost*. Cost here means harm, damage or the loss or destruction of something valued. This can be the loss of something actually in existence (and therefore capable of being possessed) or of something that would have existed or had a high probability of existing, had the event not happened. In the latter case, we are speaking of virtual loss, the loss of wealth or assets of some kind that *would* have existed, but *would not* if the event came to pass. This description makes it sound purely hypothetical, but, in many cases, virtual loss is a serious and important category. Normal procedure is to allow for such a loss (the forgone growth in asset value or profits, for example) but to apply a discount to it, to reflect the uncertainty of the future. The cost of a risk for actuarial or insurance purposes is arrived at by multiplying the probability of the event happening by the estimated size of the loss, which may or may not include virtual losses. The product of this operation is the value at risk. Having established what risks and values at risk are, the task is to categorise them so that different concrete risks can be compared to one another. Only once that task has been completed can we place risks into any kind of order or hierarchy. This produces an overall measurement of severity or gravity.

Setting probability to one side, there are three measurement criteria for risks. The first is *extent*, which means the number of people and the geographical area affected by the consequential loss or damage if the event happens. Here exists a straightforward scale. At one end is a risk borne only by a specific individual. If the event happens, they suffer a loss but nobody else does. Clearly, there is a continuous and linear progression from that point with the number of people increasing steadily. We can, if we wish, subdivide that progression using a numerical yardstick such as orders of magnitude of a base number such as ten. The end point might appear to be when the entire global population bears a cost, making the risk universal or global. In fact, that is not the terminus. Beyond the point of a loss suffered by all human beings currently alive is the prospect of a loss suffered by a given number of people not yet born, which can extend to all human beings who could possibly exist in the future, given reasonable assumptions (such as the average span of existence for the typical species). Arguably, the extent can also go so far as to include non-human species or the natural environment, with a similar scale in terms of small numbers up to entire species or, even at the ultimate extent, all species. Extent also means literal physical extent, as well as numerical. Here the scale runs from purely local, affecting only a very small area, to global, affecting the entire planet or the entire biosphere.

The second criterion is the *scale* of the damage or loss incurred if the event takes place. This ranges from the trivial to the catastrophic. At one end of the scale, the harm or loss amounts to little more than inconvenience. At the other end of the scale, it is the loss of everything that is valuable to the loss-bearer. This is captured in the distinction between loss and ruin (Taleb 2018). In monetary terms, this is like losing some amount of money, either large or small, versus losing your entire net worth. In terms of investment returns, the scale goes from a minor loss to one which wipes out so much there is no possibility of ever recovering the losses and you are left permanently impoverished. At a personal level, the cost of an accident (the risk, in this case) could range from minor injury to serious injury bringing permanent impairment or death. Here again, loss can be virtual as well as actual – to lose anticipated and expected future income is a loss, for example, even if it does not hurt as much as losing physical property or cash in the bank. A common notion is that the worst kind of loss would be one's death, but that is only true if you have no feeling for fellow human beings. For most people, having their children die is worse than their own death. By extension, the death of others around you including everyone in the community of which you are a part and ultimately the extinction of the human species is much worse than one's own death. Part of this is the condemnation to non-existence of the future people who would have otherwise lived, including one's own descendants (MacAskill 2022).

The third criterion is that of *duration*. Here the question is one of how long-lasting the damage or loss is and of how easily and quickly it can be made good. The scale ranges from brief and easily reparable to permanent and irreversible. This criterion is often combined with the second (the scale of the damage or loss incurred) to give a single criterion of the severity of damage/cost, since serious and large-scale loss will also very likely be long-lasting and hard to reverse. The most obvious example is that of death or permanent impairment where the duration of the harm (permanent) is a major feature of the size of the loss. Similarly, catastrophic loss or ruin almost always means loss that cannot be recovered or made good, at least not within a humanly meaningful timescale. Most models of types of risk, therefore, have a single criterion of severity that combines scale/intensity and duration. However, it does make sense to separate the two, even if that division is fuzzy, because thinking about duration is important in calculating payoffs for various strategies when dealing with risks and is important if we are to take virtual costs into account as well as concrete or crystallised ones. Payoffs in this context mean both positive and negative payoffs. In addition, the two variables are not perfectly aligned – it is possible to have trivial harms that are permanent or severe ones that are short-lived. An example of the first would be a minor scar or perhaps losing part of a finger. An example of the second would be a large monetary loss that is quickly made up.

Putting these three criteria together, whether as two ultimate variables or three, produces a clear structure for the classification of risks and enables us to understand what is meant by risks that are simultaneously global, catastrophic and permanent or long-lasting. The easiest way to think about this is to have two axes and variables: extent and severity (while remembering that severity is actually the product of two separate variables). The vertical axis will measure severity while the horizontal axis will measure extent. This produces a number of categories of risk, depending on how finely the two axes are subdivided. The person most associated with this analytical framework is the Oxford philosopher Nick Bostrom, who used it to arrive at a typology of GCRs (Bostrom 2002). In Bostrom's model, reproduced here, there are three levels of extent: *individual* (affecting a single person), *local* (affecting anything between a small number of people/very local area and a significant but not majority part of the planet's surface and population) and *global* (affecting the entire planet and its inhabitants). These are combined with two levels of severity, which Bostrom calls *endurable* and *terminal*. These two latter categories combine intensity and duration, since an endurable risk is one that gives rise to low levels of loss and is not long-lasting, while a terminal risk is one that brings very costly and permanent loss. As seen in Table 1, this produces six types of risk through the combinations of three values for one variable and two for the other. GCRs are listed in the upper right cell.

Bostrom's categories of endurable and terminal correspond to those of minor and catastrophic, or loss and ruin.

Risks of intermediate extent for Bostrom mean risks that impact only part of the planet's surface and population, such as an economic collapse or war affecting a single country or at most a continent. A global risk obviously means it affects the global population and entire planet. The idea of a terminal risk is worth elaborating upon. Death is the most obvious, and at the intermediate level means something like the genocide of an entire people, or a biological disaster that wipes out all or almost all of the population of a significant portion of the planet. An example of the latter would be the epidemics of diseases such as smallpox and measles that killed most of the indigenous population of the Americas after these diseases were brought there by Europeans.

Table 1

	Personal	Local	Global
Terminal	Death, death of family, permanent impairment	Genocide, local nuclear war, post-Columbus epidemics	Global nuclear war, Black Death or higher-level pandemic
Endurable	Injury	Local conventional war, natural disaster, local epidemic	Global depression, conventional world war, Covid-19

However, death, whether individual or collective, is not the only kind of terminal risk. For Bostrom and other authors, it also includes any risk that permanently forecloses future possibilities of flourishing (Ord 2020). At the individual level, this could be permanent disability. At both the individual and intermediate level, it would also include slavery or sustained and indefinite tyranny. Very importantly, it also includes a permanent (irrecoverable) breakdown of the complex systems that we call civilisation, because that would preclude for the indefinite future a whole range of scientific and technological developments, as well as economic ones, and so eliminate an enormous range of future possible human flourishing, some at least of which is predictable (i.e. we can be fairly sure it would have happened but for the event). This means, therefore, that global risks which are terminal or catastrophic are of two kinds: those that would mean human extinction or the destruction of life on Earth, and those that would bring about the complete and irretrievable collapse of civilisation, or a permanent end to progress and development.

Bostrom's work is very useful because it produces a hierarchy of risks and a clear idea of what counts as a GCR. In this schema, a GCR is an event of global extent that would, if it happens, result in permanent and severe costs for the entire population of the planet, including future generations. This could be something that results in human extermination, or something as close to that as to make no difference, or something that permanently forecloses the future development and flourishing of humanity. The philosopher Toby Ord (2021) has been particularly exercised by this last point and has explored it in a number of places. What this means is that a GCR is distinct from something that has a catastrophic effect but does not affect the whole world or radically impair the future prospects of humanity as a whole (e.g. the post-Columbian epidemics that devastated the Americas but left the Old World untouched) or from something that impacts the whole world but does not cause a loss amounting to ruin or catastrophe – a global economic depression, a worldwide conventional war or the Covid-19 pandemic would all fall into that category. This means that the category of risks which count as GCRs is more limited and defined than we might imagine and we can discuss this in a more precise and focused way than if we were simply talking about 'something big and really bad'. (For an alternative definition to the one offered by Ord and Bostrom, see Avin et al. (2018).)

That said, it is worth refining Bostrom's original model in some ways, as he himself has done (Bostrom and Cirkovic 2012: ch. 1). One is by splitting the category of 'endurable' into two, which we might call 'endurable and minor' (imperceptible or trivial) and 'endurable but severe'. The reason is that risks which are not fully catastrophic or terminal can still have very extensive and long-lasting effects as well as being terminal for large numbers of people and for a considerable range of future possibilities. In addition, the border between terminal and 'endurable but severe' is a matter of judgement in some cases. Most importantly, though, many of the events that do count as GCRs are more severe or larger-scale versions of ones that fall into the 'endurable but severe' category and therefore derive from the same underlying cause or phenomenon. This means that acting to protect against one risk may also protect against another risk. In terms of the table of types of risk, this means three rows rather than two.

We can also add another category to severity by bringing in the concept of permanent or at least multi-generational effects. This incorporates the third criterion of duration and brings virtual losses, the non-existence of things that would have existed, or might have existed, into play. This means four categories on the vertical axis, from endurable and minor to permanent. The result, as Table 2 shows, is twelve categories. The four shaded boxes are those we need to consider, in particular the two boxes at the top of the global column: global catastrophic risks, as defined earlier, and global existential risks (GERs), which are an especially severe subset of the wider set of GCRs. So, that brings us back to the question of the probability of an event happening and in particular the probability of an event happening that is both global and terminal – clear thinking about statistics and probability is required.

Table 2

	Personal	Local	Global
Multi-generational/ permanent	Death of family	Genocide, part of world made permanently uninhabitable	Human extinction, GERs
Terminal	Death	Post-Columbian epidemics, civilisational collapses	End of all civilisations, GCRs
Endurable and severe	Severe injury, permanent disablement	Civil war, economic crisis	World war, severe global depression
Endurable and minor	Minor injury	Local recession, violence	Global recession
	Personal	Local	Global

2 CATASTROPHIC RISKS AND PROBABILITY

The point to grasp is that for catastrophic or ruinous risks many ways of thinking about probability do not apply. Two ideas should be considered initially. The first has to do with the *range of values* that a variable can have and the pattern and repetition of that range over time. This relates to risk because the range of values that a risk can have is a function of the probability of a given scale of harm happening if the risk happens. The second has to do with the *nature of the risk bearer* and whether it should be understood as a singular entity or an ensemble or collective.

In many cases, a variable (e.g. the price of a commodity) can have a range of values and will have different values at different points in time. Over time, the value will fluctuate through all of the possibilities in a range. Typically, the extreme ends of the range will occur less often than those clustered around the mean (average) of the experienced range, and, critically, the value of the variable will go through the entire range repeatedly over a long enough period of time. The mean may shift, but the accumulation of data points will give us increasing certainty as to where it is and where future values of the variable are most likely to fall. That means probabilities can be assigned to future possible values, with those departing from the historical mean less probable than those that fall within a certain distance from it.

By contrast, other kinds of variable exist, whereby if a certain value comes up, then the entire process stops and the variable has no future values to consider. Here, the stop to the process of moving through the range of values may come after a determinate time, but often it is unpredictable and can happen at any point. This relates to the point about the nature of the risk bearer, which is the difference between probability or risk for a singular entity as opposed to an ensemble or collection. The most popular explanation of this distinction has been provided by Nassim Nicholas Taleb (2017). Suppose you have a hundred people who all go to the casino and gamble at the same time. One of them at least will lose everything, but that will be matched by winnings for others. The group or ensemble as a whole will not experience the fate of bankruptcy. If the trip to the casino is repeated regularly, then the overall balance of losses or returns to the ensemble will fluctuate through a range, and with enough repetitions will go through every state within that range more than once. Individual players will go bankrupt or win big, but the ensemble as a whole will not. A key point here is that the hundred is not the same hundred every time – there is a constantly shifting cast of members. That means it is not a singular collective entity; it is only an ensemble.

By contrast, suppose that you have a single person, call him Joe, who goes to the casino every day over a long period of time. Some days he wins; some days he loses. On each visit, there is a low but definite possibility that he will lose everything and be bankrupted. Sooner or later, that will happen. We cannot know exactly how many trips it will take for those odds to play out, but given enough trips it is certain to do so. When it does, even if it is after only a few visits, that is the end – there are no further visits to the casino. At this point, we exist in the second scenario – the cycling of values for the variable of wins or losses has stopped. The key point here is that the singular entity does not have to be an actual individual – that simply makes the example easier. A group of people, even a large one, can be thought of as a singular entity like Joe if two conditions are met: the connections of some kind between the individuals are sufficiently strong, and the results of certain values occurring (risks being realised) will fall upon all.

In the case of a singular entity not only do some risks being realised mean that the process has come to a full stop, but it also means that the point at which that happens cannot be predicted with any confidence from the previous history of fluctuations in value. For Taleb's second example – the single gambler repeatedly going to the casino – the amount of data about average wins and losses that can be accumulated before his last, terminal visit tells us nothing, because on that last visit he loses all of his assets plus any accumulated winnings. The difference here is the way that the different values are distributed, which tells us something about the probability of any particular value coming to pass. To get that right, however, we need to know how the quantities of the thing being measured are distributed.

This has clear application to considerations of GCR. A catastrophic or terminal risk is one that brings the human story or civilisation, at least, to a final, permanent stop. The distinction between local and global can be explained as follows. If, for example, an epidemic were to wipe out the entire human population of Australia, that would be terminal for that population, but we can expect that in a short period of time, the continent would be repopulated. If the epidemic were to affect the entire planet, that would not be the case. This brings us to the second point, which we will also return to later. When the world was sufficiently unconnected and its inhabitants separated by distance and the time taken to travel, the human world as a whole could be thought of as being like the hundred people visiting the casino. When the world and its inhabitants become sufficiently connected and interactive that we can reasonably think of them as a single entity, then they are like the single person, and this changes the way we should think about risk dramatically.

The third aspect of the probability of a GCR that we need to consider follows on from the point just made about the difficulty of predicting some kinds of terminal risk that end a sequence or process. This has to do with the way the probabilities of certain outcomes are distributed. The key is to think about that probability as being a tail-end risk: one that is in the tail-end of a probability distribution. In other words, catastrophic risks are normally low-probability events, located in the tails. This should be reassuring. If the probability is low enough, then we should not think about such risks at all, much less lose any sleep over them. Quite simply, it is not worth incurring costs through worrying about or taking action about an event that has a vanishingly small chance of happening. Even if the chance is non-trivial, if it is still low, then the chance of it happening in any one year will be low, a fraction of 1 per cent. This means that such events are infrequent, which is why, for example, an event with a 1 per cent probability of happening in any one year is described as a 'hundred-year event', meaning you should over a long period expect one such event every century on average.

We should abandon such insouciance. Risks are not so simple, for reasons we will examine, and this is true for risks of all kinds but especially for GCRs. Moreover, even if we were justified in having an attitude of confidence or fatalism with regard to such risks even as recently as a hundred years ago, that is no longer the case. For all kinds of reasons, the numbers and varieties of GCR that we have to consider are increasing (Schneier 2015). Even more alarmingly, events of this kind are more likely than we might imagine and are very hard to assign a probability to in a straightforward way and, in any event, the probability of some kinds of GCR is steadily increasing (Turchin and Denkenberger 2018; Ord 2021). Moreover, it is worth abandoning here the views of popular so-called experts and looking at the way ordinary people behave in everyday matters. This shows that ordinary people take low-probability but catastrophic events seriously. It also shows that there is a collective response to such risks that is usually characterised as 'panic', implying irrationality and overreaction. This is a mistaken way of labelling it,

because although on an individual basis such an evalua-
tion makes sense, when viewed from a longer evolutionary
perspective, it is perfectly sensible, in fact a survival trait.

So, a catastrophic risk is one where the event, should it
happen, would lead to severe and possibly terminal consequences. Such events are low probability; they are unlikely
to happen. Despite this, ordinary people regularly take
steps to insure or hedge against such low-probability but
devastating events. An example is house-rebuilding insurance. This provides that should your house be completely
destroyed so that it needs to be rebuilt entirely, from the
foundations up, the insurance will cover the cost of a like-
for-like replacement. The chances of this happening are
very low, and yet it would be very foolish not to have such
insurance. Why? Because if it did happen, your life would
be totally ruined. However, the cost of protecting against
it is low (given the low probability of the insurance pro-
vider having to pay out), and so on balance it makes sense
to take out such insurance.

This means that in most cases the expected return of
the premia, narrowly defined, is negative because the
money paid out is lost with nothing in return. However,
you do have peace of mind (not an inconsequential good),
and if the low-probability event does happen and your
house is destroyed, you get the enormous benefit of being
completely protected. To return to an example given earlier, if we calculate that the chance of an event is 1 per cent
(making it a hundred-year-event) but the consequences
of that event are ruin, then we would be foolish to ignore
it. In that case, we are dealing with a possible event with

a well-defined probability, because the chances of it happening to any one person in the future can be reasonably predicted from past experience. It is a tail-end risk in a normal distribution, one with a definite mean produced by the sum of a large number of particular cases and where the degree to which any individual case is going to depart from that mean (the variance) is known and knowable.

What, though, with risks that are disastrous, having ruinous effects, but are not so predictable? Again, these are widespread, and people have ways of dealing with them. The most widely known example is portfolio risk. This is when an unlikely event (such as a sudden and unexpected currency movement, for example, or a major and unanticipated geopolitical event) causes a fall in the value of a whole spectrum of different kinds of asset. If severe enough, it can lead to financial ruin, as in the case of the uninsured house. The challenge here is that events of this kind are much more difficult to assign a probability to – in some cases, impossible. The reason is that you cannot arrive at a firm estimation of the probability from the accumulation of data from past events, because the bulk of the events occur in a small number of major disasters.

For example, working out the probability of a house being destroyed by a specific and particular earthquake or tsunami cannot be arrived at by looking at the accumulation of the individual cases of the destruction of houses, because almost all of these happen together, as the result of a small number of massively destructive tremors. Because the number of such massively destructive tremors is low, there are not enough cases to work out a probability of any one tremor being a catastrophic one, using the law of large numbers. You may still arrive at a probability in such a case, but it will be uncertain, and if you try to do this using the kind of distribution just described, you will underestimate the probability. That is because events of this kind (house destruction in this example) do not often happen in a normal distribution. They normally happen in a power distribution where a small number of instances of one variable account for the overwhelming majority of instances of the other. Thus, a small number of the total number of currency movements cause the great majority of consequential monetary losses.

Such a distribution is said to be 'fat-tailed'. The best known such distribution is the 80:20 one in retail, for example, where the rule is that 20 per cent of customers account for 80 per cent of revenue – this means that losing the business of one of the 20 per cent is much more consequential than losing the business of one of the 80 per cent (Koch 2022). Frequently, the distribution is even more skewed. An example of that would be crime and criminals, where about 5 per cent of convicted criminals commit about 50 per cent of recorded crimes.[1] The point is that what you do not do is disregard the minority of cases of one variable that produce the great majority of cases of the other variable because they are outliers. In fact, you need to focus on them because of their impact and importance. In crime policy, for example, it makes no sense to look at the

---

1 Power law distribution and solving the crime problem. *Police Chief Magazine*, 2011 (https://www.policechiefmagazine.org/power-law -distribution-and-solving-the-crime-problem/).

great majority of people convicted of a crime, because they only account for 10 per cent of all crime; you need rather to focus on the 10 per cent of criminals who are responsible for almost all crimes. Similarly with harmful risks, the ones to think seriously about are the rare but catastrophic ones because on a historical scale they account for most of the damage.

There are ways of hedging against fat-tail risks. At the individual level, this means taking such risks more seriously than the statistically naive do. The positive defensive measure is to have some kind of protective investment or spending that will have a large positive payoff as compensation if the event happens, or to arrange things deliberately so that the consequences of such a rare event are less severe (even though this will impose costs), or to take actions that will reduce the probability of the event in the first place. The same is true at the collective level. A common response is to say that people take low-probability risks too seriously and attach an unwarranted significance to them. This is sometimes seen as a departure from pure rationality, produced by a cognitive bias such as excessive loss or risk aversion. In this case, we suggest the reaction of ordinary people is the correct one – taking low-probability but catastrophic risks more seriously than their apparent probability is a survival trait.

Let us look at a thought experiment that illustrates this. Suppose you are shown a very large roulette wheel and are told that it will be spun repeatedly. One of the numbers on the wheel, should it come up, will result in your own death and those of everyone you care about. You can tell from the size of the wheel that the chances of that specific number coming up on any one spin is low, but you do not know exactly how low. The point is that given enough turns of the wheel, the number *will* come up, and if it does, you will have lost everything. The sensible reaction is to assume that the risk while still low is higher than a simple calculation would suggest. The cost of doing this will be low, whereas the cost of underestimating it will be devastating. Moreover, sooner or later it *will* come up, so you also need to try to find a way out of the entire situation. The same is true at a collective level, and this is not simply a matter of treating a collective such as a species as being analytically a single entity (even though that does make sense in some ways). Individual responses can make sense at a collective level when enough individuals aggregate to a collective even species-wide response.

For example, take a herd of wildebeest. Each individual wildebeest has an instinctive response of flight if it detects a threat such as a nearby lion. It helps for the flight response to be easily triggered because that means the lion has less chance of getting close. This makes sense as a survival trait even if there are many false flights because there is less chance of becoming the lion's lunch. In addition, wildebeest react by fleeing when they see another one nearby fleeing. This can lead to a mass stampede as a reaction spreads through what is often an enormous herd. You might say this action is foolish and illustrates a problem of collective panic (a stampede in this case) arising out of individuals reacting to the response of a few others who may not even be responding to a serious threat. Even if they are, the chance that the lion will eat an animal on the other side of the herd is minuscule, so the wildebeest located even a moderate distance away from the one that flees originally should ignore it and keep on eating grass.

Actually, the collective stampede response makes perfect sense for the herd (and by extension the species) as a whole, which is why evolution has selected for it, at the level of the individual wildebeest. The threat that panics the instigator may be something common and limited, such as a lion or hyena. However, apart from the reality that a pack predator such as a hyena will kill far more than the original individual, the first panicked wildebeest may be responding to a different kind of threat, such as a savannah fire or a sudden flood. These threaten the entire herd, and so the chain reaction leading to a mass stampede also protects the herd as a whole against rare but large-scale and devastating risks. If they did not react this way, then most of the time the herd as a whole would be all right but, sooner or later, an event such as a fire would occur that would wipe out the entire herd.

It is therefore sensible for us to be concerned with the challenge of low-probability but catastrophic risks. But there is a tendency to underestimate the chances of such a risk coming to pass if we misunderstand the evidence we have by fitting it into an inappropriate distribution and assuming a certain consequent probability for an extreme event. The link here is that it is easy to conflate or confuse two criteria that are different. The first is the probability of an event of a certain kind happening. The second is the probability that it will have a certain kind of effect (using the metric described in the previous chapter). Take a topical example, pandemics. Suppose that in a century you have had nine pandemics and these have led to the deaths of the following numbers of people (in millions) – 12, 6, 21, 8, 11, 9, 10, 7 and 16. You would conclude on that basis that the most probable death rate for any pandemic given the mean of the death rates of the series of pandemics is 11.1 million. Suppose then that there is a tenth pandemic and that this one kills a billion people. (By comparison, the Black Death killed about a third of the planetary population by a conservative estimate, which would be 2.3 billion today.) That means that one pandemic amounts to almost all of the deaths from that cause. The average number of deaths for the series is then entirely determined by the extreme case (or as near as makes no difference). In that example, if you had looked at a much longer timespan, you would realise that the distribution of deaths from pandemics is highly fat-tailed, and so you cannot predict the likely number of deaths from any particular one from near past experience, even that of the last century.

In the absence of such an extreme case in the data (or if it is disregarded), the common practice is to use the notion of standard deviation to determine the probability of a rare event in one of the tails. The problem is that if you use the mean you obtain from assuming a normal distribution, you will arrive at an estimate of the chances of a tail-end risk happening, and of the impact of such an event, that is lower than it should be, possibly much lower. This means that in a fat-tailed distribution, you cannot use the idea of standard deviation from the mean number of deaths to determine how probable a future pandemic causing a certain number of deaths is, and if you do use that method, you will come up with a severe underestimate. In this case, the chance of a pandemic happening is the time period divided by the number of events (so if it was ten in a century, then there would be a probability to the best of our knowledge of 10 per cent in any given year), but the probability of any one pandemic causing a given number of deaths is very hard to calculate because *that* distribution is highly fat-tailed.

Given the results, as with the wildebeest, it pays to be cautious – a 0.3 per cent chance of an event that kills an eighth of the world's population, for example, is far too high, and an indeterminate chance is in some ways even more alarming (De Cecco and Orlando 2020). To take the wildebeest analogy further, the panic phase is typically short-lived as the realisation spreads through the herd that the source of the stampede is not a herd-threatening event. At that point, the wildebeest return to placid grazing. If it *is* a major threat, then the stampede continues. This means that the correct response to something like the emergence of a pandemic or the realisation of a possible GCR is to panic initially and take steps that will prevent or significantly mitigate the possible worst-case outcome and to only 'calm down' once it becomes clear that the risk does not lie within the terminal category (Sunstein 2006).

Finally, as we shall shortly see, the probabilities of certain kinds of event happening and of those events having catastrophic results are increasing. In some cases, this is happening in a cumulative way, with a progression of events making a disastrous event steadily more likely (Turner 2014). At the same time, new kinds of risk have appeared or become at least seriously conceivable. Overall, this means that the chance of some kind of GCR happening is growing. This diversion into probability raises a matter we shall return to – the misguided way of thinking of many people, especially economists.

Having defined what we mean by a global catastrophic risk in theory, and said something about the problems these risks raise for naive probability theorising, what about the content? What are examples of a GCR? Given what we have said, how might we grade these in terms of both concern and tractability? And why is concern about them on the rise right now?

3   THE RISE OF CONCERN ABOUT GLOBAL CATASTROPHIC RISKS

Many serious-minded, intelligent people are now very worried about GCRs, to the extent, in some cases, of devoting their professional lives to the subject (Chivers 2020). The topic itself is not a new one. Narratives of catastrophes that destroy the world are found in most human cultures as the many myths of an all-destroying flood show. (There are others, such as the Aztec accounts of the world being destroyed by solar changes.) The idea of an apocalypse, a sudden and climactic sweeping away of all that is, which brings an end to history, appears to be a human universal. It probably starts from extending the awareness of the inevitability of one's own death to encompass wider categories such as one's community, all human beings or even the entire world. It plays a central part in monotheistic religions, where the end of the world is described in great detail: one feature is that the end will come suddenly and unexpectedly 'like a thief in the night'. This means that although we may know it is coming, we have no way of knowing *when* it will come, which could be any time from tomorrow into the distant future. There will, though, be warning signs, but most will not recognise them at the time until the end is upon us. Rather facetiously we might add that, in the case of Christianity, the event will have an infinite payoff – infinitely positive for some and infinitely negative for others.

For most of history, accounts of this kind were found in myth, revealed writings, and the commentaries they inspired. They were not a feature of fiction or even of philosophy, much less scientific argument. In the modern world, and particularly since the later nineteenth century, accounts of disasters that bring an end to human civilisation or even cause the extermination of the human race have become common. One early example is M. P. Shiel's *The Purple Cloud* (1929), in which a mysterious cloud of gas wipes out all humanity apart from one survivor. Sometimes the narrative is set after such an event, while the event itself remains mysterious – one of the first examples of this is *After London or Wild England* by Richard Jefferies (1885). Both of these novels can be seen as belonging to the emergent genre of science fiction or speculative fiction, and as that genre has developed, accounts of the catastrophic end of the world or civilisation, or of the world and human life after such an event, have become a staple feature (Wagar 1982).

In addition, several speculative but non-fictional works have explored the first intimations of catastrophic risks and the future of civilisation. For obvious reasons these became popular just after the Great War. H. G. Wells produced several of these types of work, as well as several fictional works. An interesting feature of Wells's works was that they combined dire warnings of possible disaster with excited anticipation of glorious futures – provided the right people were in charge. (This is a recurring theme in speculative non-fiction.) More often, the two kinds of speculation came from different authors. One example is the deliberately paired works *Daedalus*, by J. B. S. Haldane (published first, 1924), and *Icarus*, by Bertrand Russell (a riposte, also published in 1924) – the Haldane work posited a future in which human knowledge increased to the point where humanity gained control over its own evolutionary destiny, while Russell argued that such power would almost certainly be misused, with catastrophic results.

The reason that consideration of such matters moved from the realms of myth and theology to both fictional and serious speculation was the sudden explosion of scientific and technological knowledge, and the transformation of the world to what we call modernity. Faced with this, various people extrapolated current trends into the future and wondered whether the trends of ever-increasing knowledge and control of the physical world would have benign or disastrous results. The two world wars also made people increasingly aware of the destructive power and potential of modern science and machine production, while modern totalitarianism created a whole new category of tyranny to worry about. Simultaneously, the modern environmental movement, which took shape in the last two decades of the nineteenth century as a minority movement, became alarmed and concerned by the human impact on the natural world, now more visible, rapid and extensive than before. All of this combined with the long-standing idea of an apocalypse to create a new focus for unease and anxiety.

This anxiety remained a matter for speculation as opposed to serious scientific investigation until 1945 (Moynihan 2020), when the world saw two nuclear attacks on Japan at the end of World War II. It became clear to many that for the first time ever human beings had the technological capacity to destroy civilisation and maybe even all human life. That year also saw the founding of the first organisation concerned with the problem of GCRs, the *Bulletin of the Atomic Scientists*. Set up by former participants in the Manhattan Project, it was originally a magazine. It acted as a platform for research into the issues surrounding nuclear weapons, the arms race that had been going on even before the first nuclear test (unknown to many at the Project and in the US who believed that their security was tight enough to ensure nobody else would obtain a nuclear weapon any time soon), and the threat that these posed to the future of humanity and life on Earth. This was reflected in the best known symbol of the *Bulletin*, the Doomsday Clock, with its hands set just before midnight and the shifting closeness to that time reflecting the organisation's judgement as to how probable the threat of a nuclear apocalypse was and is. Over the years, the time has shifted back and forth; originally set at seven minutes to midnight, it now stands at 90 seconds. This is the closest it has ever been, the furthest away being seventeen minutes in 1991. Over the years, the organisation has expanded its concerns to a much wider variety of existential and catastrophic risks, although nuclear weapons remain its primary interest.

Initially, the *Bulletin* was a bit of an outlier – nuclear weapons, and the threat of nuclear war, was its main novel GCR of concern, and in that area the *Bulletin* soon established itself as the dominant voice. Its considered and analytical approach set it apart from more political movements to abolish nuclear weapons and the many examples of the continued fascination for narratives of catastrophe and collapse found in science fiction. The difference from earlier and continuing forms of speculative non-fiction was the attempt to think seriously about probability of disaster such as nuclear war and to explore more fully and in a quantified way what its consequences might be. The Doomsday Clock captured this. The authors of the essays published in the *Bulletin* did not simply warn that a nuclear war was a catastrophe to be avoided; they tried to work out exactly how great the risk or probability of such an event was, whether it was increasing or diminishing, and exactly how extensive the effects would be. This fits into the systematic thinking about risk we have already discussed.

The clock, and its timing, was a vivid pictorial representation. One very important point is that the time on the clock has never been meant to be a prediction: it has always been a reflection of a judgement about the *possibility* of something happening, not a *prediction* as to *how soon* it may happen. This distinction, between calculating probability and making predictions, is an important one analytically, which we will return to.

During the 1960s, other issues and questions about GCR began to emerge and new voices began to appear, focusing on progressive environmental degradation and resource exhaustion. These were connected in many cases by an underlying alarm about population growth and derived from a suddenly resurgent Malthusianism, which dated back to 1948 and the publication of Fairfield Osborn's *Our Plundered Planet* (1948) and William Vogt's *Road to Survival* (1948). This upsurge started with works such as Rachel Carson's *Silent Spring* (1962) and Paul Ehrlich's *The Population Bomb* (1968). The culmination of this early wave of concern about a range of GCRs was the Club of Rome's *Limits to Growth*, published in 1972 (Meadows et al. 1972), which was an exercise in trying to work out what possible futures would be like if certain policies were followed (and trends either arrested or allowed to continue), given a number of underlying assumptions. One of the central messages of the work was that if certain trends continued, the chances of a catastrophic collapse of the global system would increase until a tipping point was reached. At that point, the collapse would happen, very abruptly. This brings to mind Hemingway's famous account of how bankruptcy happens – slowly and then suddenly.

Following the publication of *Limits to Growth*, the 1970s saw the first major concern about a possible serious collapse of civilisation (in the sense that its proponents thought it was a real possibility, even a probability) that was founded upon scientific argument rather than religious thought or myth. Crucially, as with the *Bulletin*, a key element was an attempt to estimate the likely chance of a global collapse. However, this first peak of interest and concern was not sustained. Increasingly, there was serious pushback, both intellectually and politically, which took the form of critical works such as Wilfred Beckerman's *In Defence of Economic Growth* (with added force because of Beckerman's generally left-wing position) (1974; see also Beckerman 1996).

There was, initially, a lack of effective response by the catastrophists to these criticisms so that by the 1980s the first wave of both environmentalism in general and concern about catastrophic risks had faded. There was instead a renewed focus on innovation and economic growth as the keys to improvements in the human condition. Individuals such as Donella Meadows and Lester Brown continued to make the argument, and some of the institutions set up earlier survived, such as the Worldwatch Institute and the Whole Earth Catalog, but they were holdouts (see Meadows et al. 1992; Meadows and Randers 2004).

One aspect of this debate is that both sides focused on systems critique, extrapolations and linear thinking to generate forecasts – they did not make risk calculations. When thinking of the longer term, this way of thinking does not allow for extreme events and their impacts. Examples include major natural disasters, revolutions, major economic crises, or sudden and unanticipated scientific or technological discoveries (Cole 1973). Events of this kind can be altogether unexpected or they can be known about but difficult to predict with accuracy. Such events may bring major costs or major benefits, or even a mixture of both (as the Black Death did, for example). There are also 'white swans', events that we know are going to happen with near certainty but do not know when.

Confronted with this, predictive forecasts are dangerous. In thinking about possible threats and existential threats, we need to think like an intelligent gambler (Duke 2018). We need first to identify threats that, if they were to happen, would have massive negative results. Second, we need to try to work out, using proper probability reasoning, what the likely probability of those events is. At that point we have to consider whether the risk is acceptable, and if not, what can be done about it. We also need to address the question: 'If, despite all we do, X does happen, what then? Is there a way to mitigate that impact, to hedge it?' The more recent thinking about GCRs follows *this* model (Bostrom and Cirkovic 2012).

Concern about possible catastrophic risks of a global scale began to reappear in the first decade of this century. Not coincidentally, this was about the time that interest in radical technological breakthrough and the idea of a 'singularity' also broke out of the small subculture to which it had previously been confined. One work that attracted attention was the 2003 book by the then Astronomer Royal and future President of the Royal Society, Sir Martin Rees, with the arresting title *Our Final Century* and the prediction that the human species only had an even-money chance of making it to the twenty-second century. Richard Posner published a comprehensive work *Catastrophe: Risk and Response* (2004), which was notable because as an economist he used cost–benefit analysis to argue for both the severity of the threat of catastrophic events and the benefits and reasonableness of taking action to prevent or mitigate these – something other economists dissent from – and made the case for GCRs to be a prominent policy concern. In 2008, a conference on the topic was held at Oxford University, with the papers subsequently being published in a collection edited by Nick Bostrom and Milan Cirkovic (2012). The most recent notable addition to a growing literature is the work *The Precipice* by the philosopher Toby Ord (2020). As well as academics, several leading figures from the world of hi-tech industry and Silicon Valley have been actively involved in supporting institutions that explore the issue. These include Peter Thiel and Elon Musk.

The array of organisations researching possible catastrophic risks is also impressive. One of the first was the Machine Intelligence Research Institute, set up in 2000. It was followed by the Nuclear Threat Initiative (2001), the Lifeboat Foundation (2009), the Global Catastrophic Risks Institute (2011), Global Challenges Foundation, the Cambridge-based Centre for the Study of Existential Risk (2012), the Future of Life Institute (2014) and the Center on Long-Term Risk (2016). A key event was the creation of the Future of Humanity Institute at Oxford University in 2005, with Nick Bostrom a leading figure. As well as this and the Cambridge centre, other university-based organisations included the Millennium Alliance for Humanity and the Biosphere at Stanford, set up soon after 2000, and the Center for Security and Emerging Technology at Georgetown University, created in 2019. There are differences in emphasis between the various organisations and the individuals associated with them, but certain themes recur and there is a unifying feature. They are all concerned with identifying possible GCRs and establishing, where possible, well-founded probability estimates for both them and their effects. They are following the risk-establishment model rather than forecasts.

Why, though, the sudden revival? There are two main reasons: firstly, an awareness of developments in science and technology that carry enormous risk (Smil 2012); secondly, the concerns about processes such as human impact on the biosphere and climate, which subsided during the 1970s, resurged, as growing evidence of possible massively harmful consequences of human activity became stronger.

All of this led to two conclusions: (a) human activity and inventiveness were increasing the number and variety of GCRs that might happen (Ord et al. 2010). The detonation of an atomic bomb had previously added one such risk to the list of natural cataclysms, but that has now been joined by a collection of others; and (b) some of the risks that had always existed were now becoming more probable and potentially more devastating, again because of human activity and the development of human society since the Industrial Revolution (Ravilious 2005).

The conclusion for many of those involved was that humanity as a species was in a period of unusual vulnerability, where the risk of either extinction or the irretrievable collapse of civilisation was higher than it had been for all of previous history and higher than it will be in another century or so, assuming continued technological and scientific progress.

There were now novel risks arising from new technologies, such as artificial intelligence (AI), which posed a higher chance of human extinction than the long-standing natural risks that human beings have always been exposed to. This is a continuing risk because the processes of discovery and technological innovation are continuing. The nature of the challenge was described by Bostrom in his paper on 'The vulnerable world hypothesis' (2019). He argues that we should think of scientific and technological progress as being like repeatedly pulling balls out of an opaque urn. Usually the balls are white (the technology is beneficial), occasionally they are grey (the technology has a mixture of good and bad consequences – television and electronic communication are examples), but in neither case does the technology pose an existential or catastrophic risk. However, we know that the urn contains or may contain black balls – technologies that would lead to human extinction or the irretrievable collapse of complex civilisation. We do not know how many black balls there are, which means all of the probability calculations we talked about apply. If a black ball is pulled, then it is the end of everything – no further balls will be drawn. We cannot tell from our experience so far how probable it is that the next one we draw will be a black ball. In the future, our technological capacity may have evolved to the point where we can handle unpleasant surprises, so no ball will be truly black, but we are not there yet.

Moreover, technological progress means that humans now have the capacity to end civilisation or all human life but have not yet developed the institutions and practices to deal with these risks. Economic, scientific and technological progress has currently outrun the capacity of our institutions. We also, as a species, lack the ability to foresee clearly where problems may arise in many cases and therefore the ability to think ahead about how to deal with them. Making this possible would be to make the urn in Bostrom's analogy transparent, or at least translucent, so that we would have a better idea of where the 'black balls' are. It is this that motivates the think tanks and institutes.

What makes the present historical moment one of particularly acute vulnerability is something that authors such as Ord and Bostrom overlook. They are most exercised by existential risk, the possibility of human extinction. They are less troubled by the second kind of global catastrophe, that of an irretrievable collapse of civilisation. Ord argues that this is a lesser risk because it is very difficult to permanently destroy civilisation and stop the 'civilising process' with no hope of recovery. For him, the collapse of modern civilisation would be like the end of classical ancient civilisation, a disaster but not a permanent one. There would be a dark age, but eventually it would pass. In my view this is much too sanguine, for three reasons.

First, the development process of the last 300 years has produced a human world that is so *interconnected* and *mutually reliant* that it is analytically a single entity in many ways. A catastrophe is far more likely now to be global in its impact. This means our situation is more like that of the single person going to the casino rather than the ensemble, and in terms of the collapse of civilisation, this means any such collapse would be global. There is much less chance of there being a part of the world that is less affected or escapes entirely and from which civilisation could recover and spread.

Second, modern civilisation is much more *vulnerable* than many realise. It is true that the wealth and the technological capacity we now possess enable us to deal with threats and challenges much more effectively than in the past, thus reducing the chances of catastrophe and making recovery easier. However, there are two problems here. Our wealth and capacity currently rest on a narrow foundation, as they depend upon continued access to the concentrated energy found in fossil fuels. Presently, despite much hand-waving, there are no realistic alternatives for activities that are essential to the continued flourishing of modern civilisation.

Moreover, the way modern civilisation has developed makes it more vulnerable to collapse at present, rather than less. The problem is *excessive complexity* and lack of redundancy in the systems through which the activities that make up civilisation are organised (Tainter 1990). This makes them vulnerable to catabolic collapse in the face of severe shocks. Counterintuitively, wealthy and complex societies can sometimes be more affected by natural or man-made disasters than less developed ones. An example is the Black Death, which killed about 40 per cent of the population of Eurasia, but which the Eurasian civilisations survived. If a similarly lethal pandemic were to happen today, we should bet against global civilisation surviving, because the disruption to the systems that it depends on could be so severe that they would collapse and not be able to recover. The impact of the much milder Covid-19 virus is suggestive.

The first two factors mean that a global civilisational collapse is perhaps more likely than many suppose. But it is the third factor that should really give us pause. Why should it be more likely to be *irretrievable*? The reason was first identified by Harrison Brown in his work *The Challenge of Man's Future* (1954).

Brown argued that a civilisational collapse now would be different from all previous collapses. Modern civilisation has used up all of the readily accessible energy as well as other resources that are available at low cost, leaving only those resources that can be used with advanced technology and high-energy input. That is not a problem for those living in a high-tech and high-energy civilisation. If such a civilisation should suffer a general collapse, however, any rebuilding would be extremely difficult, because any reconstruction beyond the level of a classic pre-modern agricultural civilisation would require *access to energy* that would no longer be available. The conclusion is that a civilisational collapse now would mean that while a successor one comparable to the kind of civilisation seen many times in our history, but with additional knowledge and skills, would be possible, a modern technological one would not. That would not only eliminate the range of expanded possibilities found in modernity, but it would also make all of the current future possibilities of further human development and expansion impossible.

In another century or so, we will not be as vulnerable as we are now. We should as a species have developed the practices and institutions that will enable us to handle the risk Bostrom raises. We should have developed new technologies (e.g. of energy) and ways of organising a complex world society that make it less vulnerable. The positive aspect of this is that if we make it as a species and civilisation through the next two centuries, then we can expect a very long and almost boundless future. As William MacAskill (2022) has argued, we should give all of those potential future people weight in our calculations as to what we should do here and now. That certainly makes the duty of navigating this moment of vulnerability more pressing, given the possible futures that depend upon our doing so.

4   TYPES AND EXAMPLES OF GLOBAL CATASTROPHIC RISKS

What, though, were the specific risks the scholars and entrepreneurs involved were worried about? Once GCRs have been defined, it then becomes possible to think analytically about such risks. One distinction frequently made is between anthropogenic risks and natural or non-anthropogenic risks. The former are risks that arise from human activity or processes dominated by it, including those associated with novel technologies. The latter are those that arise from the normal workings of the universe, whether that be biological, such as a naturally occurring pandemic, or physical, such as a comet or asteroid impact, or some sort of combination of the two, such as a renewal of the ice age due to fluctuations in solar activity and the dynamics of the planet's climate system.

Natural GCRs include the kinds of event that have periodically wiped out the majority of species on the planet, but, fortunately for us, such events are very rare. Very much more common are risks that are minor in terms of the geological timescale and the entire biosphere but would have a devastating effect on human populations, destroying civilisation. Concern is intense, though, with regard to anthropogenic risks because these are typically of even higher probability and, in several cases, are those where the risk is clearly increasing in terms of both the chances of an event happening and the extent and severity of the impact.

This distinction – between anthropogenic and non-anthropogenic risks – is of limited value, partly because the distinction between them is not clear cut. The possibility of active ill-will leading to disaster, or of unintended catastrophic effects of social processes, should be considered. It is useful, therefore, to divide possible GCRs into no fewer than seven categories. These are:

- Continuing natural risks
- Exacerbated or accelerated natural risks
- Misuse or consequences of novel technologies
- Global systems collapse
- Risks from human ill-will or destructiveness
- Speculative and science-fictional risks
- Unknown risk

Continuing natural (non-anthropogenic) risks

For as long as hominids have existed, there have been background threats to their continued existence as a species (McGuire 2009). In terms of Earth's geological history, there have been at least five episodes of mass extinction, defined as relatively short periods that saw a massive reduction in the diversity of plant and animal species, due to a sharp increase in the rate at which species became extinct (Brannen 2017). The most recent happened at the end of the Cretaceous Era some 66 million years ago. All kinds of hypotheses have been put forward to explain these episodes, but what does seem clear is that major extinction events occur regularly over the course of geological time. The fossil record suggests at least 25 such episodes. Given the duration of geological time, that tells us that mass extinction episodes are rare but still happen regularly, at intervals of roughly 25–30 million years.

Events of this kind clearly have natural causes and are produced by natural phenomena. There is wide agreement that the most recent one at the end of the Cretaceous was caused by a large asteroid impact on what is now the Yucatán Peninsula, the so-called Chicxulub Event. This threw enormous quantities of pulverised rock into the atmosphere and blocked out the majority of solar radiation for several years, so triggering a collapse in biodiversity that involved the extinction of most dinosaur species. In other extinction events, a common factor appears to be sustained and widespread large-scale volcanic eruptions that have caused prolonged global cooling (Benton 2003). Most biologists and zoologists believe that the world is now in a sixth major extinction event, though they see it as being primarily anthropogenic, due to the impact of human activity on the climate and the biosphere (Ceballos et al. 2015).

The two main kinds of existential natural risk therefore appear to be a major asteroid impact, comparable in scale to the Chicxulub Event, and an episode of geographically widespread and super-massive volcanism. A major asteroid impact is possible to predict using current technology and might be preventable given current technology or technologies that could be developed within the near future. But the same is not true for widespread supervolcanism; such a major geophysical process is beyond human agency.

Such phenomena are much more extensive than the eruption of a single or isolated supervolcano and are spread over a significant part of the planet's surface. The precise mechanism that causes such episodes is not understood, but they have occurred several times. They are usually termed basalt plain events, after the geological formations that are their most obvious surviving legacy. So, these huge asteroid impacts and supervolcanic eruptions are examples of events that would be impossible for human beings to deal with, given current technology.

Possible extinction-level events arise from processes happening outside the Earth itself. Discussion of such possible risks often includes phenomena that we may call cosmic risks, because they derive from the workings of the larger universe. An example of this would be a supernova in a nearby star (Bostrom and Cirkovic 2012: ch. 12), which would lead to an intense burst of gamma ray and X-ray radiation that would propagate out from the supernova and sterilise all systems within a given range. Fortunately, the chances of this are very low because such events are infrequent, even given the number of stars in the galaxy and the age of the majority of them. This means that although we can do absolutely nothing about it (so it is an existential risk we simply have to live with), the chances are that by the time it does happen, we will, barring other kinds of

GCR, have either reached a level of technology where we can do something about it, or will have spread sufficiently widely that a part of the human species will survive.

Below the level of mass extinction events, there could be repeated, more frequent natural events which would not threaten the entire planetary ecosystem but which would cause massive devastation were they to happen, almost certainly leading to the end of complex human society. Such an event is likely to be the final end of civilisation for the reasons given above on pages 44–46.

A natural risk that would be global in impact, bringing about sufficient impact to cause the collapse of complex civilisation, is therefore a risk worth taking seriously because the cost would be enormous and would certainly qualify as ruinous, while the probability, although low, is still higher than that of the major natural risks just described. There are five such natural risks, all of which are non-speculative in the sense that such events have happened in the historical or prehistoric past.

Asteroid impact

While major asteroid impacts of the kind that wiped out the dinosaurs are infrequent, the same is not true of major meteorite impacts or asteroid strikes of a smaller magnitude. The best recorded case is that of the meteor which exploded over Tunguska in 1908, flattening 830 square miles of forest with an explosive force equivalent to somewhere between 3 and 30 megatons of TNT. To put this in perspective, the meteor in question is estimated to have been about 100 metres in diameter. The Solar System has literally thousands of objects of that size or larger. The asteroid that caused the Chicxulub Event is estimated to have been about 10 km in diameter and so a hundred times larger in diameter than the Tunguska meteor, but there are many objects in near-Earth space that fall within that range. The impact of a larger body such as an object with a diameter between 500 m and 1 km would be massive. Damage would depend on the location of the impact, but the effects would be worldwide or near worldwide, and devastating. That this will happen eventually is effectively a certainty, but it is impossible to establish odds for any precise time frame (Homer 2018; Bostrom and Cirkovic 2012: ch. 11).

Supervolcanic eruption

Volcanoes and their eruptions are a regular and familiar feature of the Earth's geology. They can cause disasters such as the destruction of Pompeii in 79 AD but are by their nature localised and so not global risks. More serious is the threat of supervolcanoes (McGuire 2005; Bostrom and Cirkovic 2012: ch. 10). These are volcanic eruptions that occur when a large pool of magma from the planetary mantle bursts through the lithosphere (the planetary crust), and by definition eject at least one thousand cubic kilometres (240 cubic miles) of pulverised rock into the Earth's atmosphere. This creates a 'caldera', or crater, often so large that it is invisible at ground level and can only be discerned from altitude, or even from orbit. Sometimes, repeated eruptions have occurred at the same place, spaced out over long periods of time. The best known example of this is the caldera located underneath Yellowstone National Park in the US.

A supervolcanic eruption would have an impact over an entire continental landmass or even the whole planet, the major effect being the blocking of solar radiation and a dramatic cooling of the planet with further, consequential climatic effects, caused by this blocking of solar radiation. Of course, large volcanic eruptions that do not make it into the supervolcano category can still have very serious effects, for example, the eruption of Mount Tambora in Indonesia in 1815 lowered temperatures around the world so much that 1816 was known as 'the year without a summer'. The cold and wet conditions caused major harvest failures and outbreaks of epidemic disease such as typhus all over the world. Before that, the eruption of Mt Tarawera in New Zealand in the 1310s triggered the Great European Famine of 1315–17. In 535, an eruption in Central America led to a prolonged period of global cooling (the so-called Late Antique Little Ice Age) that, according to one view, had massive geopolitical consequences, including the final collapse of ancient civilisations (Keys 2000). A true supervolcanic eruption would be at least four times larger than any of these, and the effect correspondingly greater.

Supervolcanic eruptions are much more frequent than basalt plane creations but still rare. One has happened within the lifetime of the human species – the eruption of Lake Toba in Sumatra, roughly 71,000 years ago. According to some palaeoanthropologists, this caused climatic effects that nearly led to human extinction. According to

Ambrose (1998), the genetic and other evidence suggests a mere 3,000 to 10,000 individuals survived. (Others are sceptical.) The Lake Toba eruption was at least twelve times larger than the eruption of Mount Tambora and is estimated to have covered the whole of South Asia with a layer of volcanic ash 15 cm thick. On the one hand, a modern technological society would have the resources and capacity to deal better with such an event than an agricultural-based society. On the other hand, society's complexity would make it highly susceptible to disruption and possible collapse. The example of the eruption of the Icelandic volcano Eyjafjallajökull in April of 2010 – a very small event by the standards of supervolcanoes – shows how much disruption can be caused. A true supervolcanic eruption would have global effects and almost certainly trigger a systemic unravelling of civilisation worldwide. One estimate of the probability of such an event is that they happen on average once every million years. This estimate probably understates the likelihood of one happening in any given year, but even so this is a low-probability event.

Natural climate change

As noted, the main way that volcanic eruptions have an impact on the world and by extension on humans is through their effect on the climate. This raises the third continuing natural global catastrophic risk, which is natural (non-anthropogenic) climate change. Given the current alarm over human-instigated climate change, it is worth remembering that as recently as the 1970s many were concerned with change in the planet's climate due to natural causes. The point is that a significant and relatively abrupt change in the global climate will have significant and often damaging effects regardless of whether it is man-made or not. In the 1970s, the main worry of authors such as Nigel Calder was that there was a high probability of reversion to an ice age (Calder 1974) because normality over the last two and half million years has been for much of the Northern Hemisphere to be covered in ice. For the last 12,000 years or so, we have been living in an 'interglacial' period of greater warmth.

Crucially, the switch from an interglacial to a glacial phase is sudden and abrupt. The research indicates that this happens in a matter of a few decades at most and maybe even just one decade (Alley 2000; National Research Council 2002). In the 1970s, Calder and others were concerned that a sudden move to a new ice age was more probable than most supposed. Their argument was presented as being a forecast or prediction that an ice age was about to start, rather than a probability judgement. Perhaps for this reason, the idea has appeared as simply being wrong, whereas it was in fact entirely reasonable. And certainly, relatively sudden switches in the climate – in either direction – remain a serious threat because of their hugely disruptive effects. To better comprehend, we can look at the impact of previous periods of planetary cooling that did not reach the full level of an ice age, such as the two Little Ice Ages of the sixth and seventh centuries and the period from 1300 to 1850. The peak period of the latter, in the central decades of the seventeenth century, saw not

only widespread famines but also a cluster of political crises and civil wars, peaking in 1648 (Parker and Smith 1997;
Parker 2013).

Natural pandemics

A pressing continuing natural risk is that of a natural pandemic: a pandemic caused by a natural process of mutation
producing a new pathogen. This is the type of natural GCR
with the highest probability, on the historical evidence
(McMillen 2016). Within the last two thousand years there
have been at least three true pandemics (an epidemic that
is global in scope) at a level of severity that would make
them a GCR. Each of them carried off between a third and
a half of the global population. Two were certainly outbreaks of bubonic plague: the Black Death, which ravaged
Eurasia in two major waves during the fourteenth century,
and the Plague of Justinian, which devastated the populations of Eurasia and parts of Africa during the sixth and
seventh centuries. The third was the pandemic that killed
people right across Eurasia in the late second to middle
third century, usually known as the Antonine Plague (the
first major peak) and the Plague of Cyprian (the second).
This is suspected to have been measles or smallpox. We
might also count the huge epidemics that wiped out most
of the indigenous inhabitants of the Americas after 1492,
although here human activity played a key part, in the
shape of Columbus and subsequent Europeans bringing
Old World pathogens to the New. (Fortunately for them,
there was only one disease sent in the other direction,

which was syphilis – bad but not as devastating in demographic terms.)

It hardly needs saying that a pandemic on the same scale as Justinian's Plague or the Black Death would have a truly devastating impact. Civilisation in the widest sense could survive, but absent a number of measures, it is unlikely that modern high-energy civilisation could withstand such a shock. The risk of this is still low but several times higher than the other risks in this category and certainly worth preparing for given the effects. In addition, certain features of the way we live now (discussed further on pages 63–64) make the chance of such a pandemic much higher than the 1 in 700 years probability that history would indicate – it is more like 1 in 300 or 400 years, so 0.3 per cent in any one year (Mannheim 2018).

Carrington Events

The final continuing natural GCR worth considering is a large coronal mass ejection (CME), leading to an intense geomagnetic storm over at least half the planet, probably all of it. This happens when a large mass of plasma and an associated magnetic pulse are released from the outer layers of the Sun (the corona). These are associated in ways we do not yet understand with solar activity such as flares and the sunspot cycle. They are normal and frequent with between three and five in any 24 hour period, depending on the stage of the sunspot cycle. If sufficiently active, they have an effect on the Earth, causing effects such as the aurora borealis and the disruption of the ionosphere.

This is usually harmless. Sometimes, though, there are large CMEs that lead to very severe geomagnetic storms. The most recent took place in 1989 (there were others in 1921 and 1960) and was severe enough to disrupt electricity supply in Quebec. But the last really massive one to affect Earth was in 1859 – the so-called Carrington Event, named after the British astronomer who recorded it, Richard Carrington. It caused significant disruption to telegraph systems, but at the time, that was the only major system using electricity. A solar storm of similar size today would cause very serious disruption to electricity supplies, radio and television transmissions and the Internet, and through its electromagnetic pulse effects would damage or burn out many devices and components. Whereas in 1859 disruption to normal life was minimal, today it would be extensive – this is another example of the increased vulnerability of the modern world to severe natural events.

A Carrington Event–sized CME would thus be a major disaster. Recent research estimates the impact on the US alone to be in the range of 3.6 per cent to 15.5 per cent of annual GDP (Lloyds 2013). It would almost certainly be global in extent. Whether it would be catastrophic, in the sense of causing irreversible damage to modern civilisation, is less clear – this would depend partly on the vulnerability of the modern world to progressive systems collapse (for further details, see pages 89–92) and on the degree to which damage was permanent or excessively costly to make good. It would undoubtedly fall into at least the 'global and severe but endurable' box of Bostrom's table. If an event were to be even slightly more powerful, there would a much higher likelihood of catastrophic results. The probability of such an event is roughly on a par with that of a devastating natural pandemic at about 0.3 per cent in any year. Since 1859 there has been one solar storm of the same size as the Carrington Event, on 23 July 2012, but on that occasion, the ejected coronal mass missed the Earth. Ice core evidence shows that Earth has been hit by events of this size or larger on many occasions, such as 775, 994, 1052 and 1259, suggesting that this is a 300-year event. The 775 storm was a major one, estimated to be ten times more powerful than the Carrington Event.

All of these continuing natural GCRs are ones that have always been present; there is nothing new in them. They are also all relatively low in probability (apart perhaps from a major pandemic or a severe CME) and that probability is stable in human terms because it is determined by natural factors. This in turn points to another feature of natural GCRs: they are impossible or nearly so for human beings to prevent or avert (in the sense of reducing their future probability by actions taken now). It could be argued that anthropogenic global warming has inadvertently made a switch to a new ice age slightly less likely, but it is unlikely that even modern human activity could have an impact as significant as preventing renewed glaciation, given the forces at play. The other side to this is that there are various actions that we can take to mitigate the effects or to ensure civilisational survival in the event of one of them happening, as we shall see in the last two chapters.

Exacerbated or accelerated natural risks

As well as the kinds of natural risk that have always been there in the background, there exists a category of risks that are natural, in the sense that they are events or processes that are primarily natural in their origin or nature rather than being entirely caused by human action, but are exacerbated by human activity. That is, human activity makes it more likely that they will happen, bring a tipping point in a process much closer, or make the effects of the event more extensive than they would otherwise be. Several of the GCRs that cause the most concern fall into this category. In some sense, this is a phenomenon that can be found at every level of the second risk table in chapter 1. The impact of a hurricane, for example, is much greater in terms of the damage and disruption that it causes in a modern society as opposed to a pre-modern one, simply because there is more stuff and systems to smash up and disrupt. This is not a matter of there simply being greater monetary loss; it is that systems we now depend upon, such as electrical grids and complex distributional systems, are disrupted and damaged by major events, while the simpler systems of earlier times were not. Of course, the greater wealth of the modern world and its greater complexity also mean that we can now absorb larger shocks. However, there is a flip side to this, which we often ignore, as shown by the Carrington Event–size CMEs. In addition, other factors mean that modern societies by the way they collectively act are making certain kinds of dangers more likely and more devastating, in a way that is not simply a function of greater fragility or more being at stake. (For fragility, see the section beginning on page 88 and also pages 149–50.)

Human-created or -affected pandemics

Pandemics are a classic example of accelerated natural risk (Bostrom and Cirkovic 2012: ch. 14). The nature of the modern world makes pandemics more likely and, when they do happen, more difficult to control in the early stages. Moreover, various economic and technological changes are dramatically increasing the probability of a serious pandemic, and deliberate human action or the possibility of it may lead to a truly devastating pandemic. This is a risk where both the probability and the extent plus severity are going in the wrong direction.

In the ancient and medieval world, pandemics were massive but infrequent. They carried off a significant part of the global population but happened only once every few centuries or even more rarely. One reason was the simple lack of connections between different parts of the world. This meant that an epidemic would often be confined to a region, one that had a sufficiently dense set of trade and travel routes within it. It was only after regular trade links were established right across the Eurasian landmass that a disease could spread, albeit slowly, all the way from the Mediterranean to China. This lack of opportunities for pathogens to spread was both an advantage and a disadvantage: it meant there were fewer epidemics affecting the entire Old World, but it also meant that populations not affected by a regional outbreak would not develop resistance to it. This is one reason why, when pandemics did happen, they were so devastating. (The experience of the post-Columbus New World is an extreme example of this.)

Another reason for the rarity of pandemics in the pre-modern world was the discovery of ways of controlling and limiting the spread of epidemics, which meant that while there were many outbreaks of infectious disease such as typhus or plague, they were localised. The best example of such control was quarantine, the practice of compelling long-distance travellers such as merchants to confine themselves for a period both on arrival at their destination and on their return. This was adopted all over Eurasia in the aftermath of the Black Death and was the main reason why, although the plague remained virulent and there were many local outbreaks, there was no further pandemic outbreak of that illness until the later nineteenth century, and despite weaknesses in medical knowledge, which meant that people had no accurate theoretical understanding of why these measures worked.

By contrast to the pre-modern situation, since 1815 there have been around twenty genuine pandemics, including no fewer than seven cholera pandemics. Suddenly, they have become much more frequent and therefore probable, even though we have not yet experienced a major one.

The fact that none of these has been of the most severe kind, however, highlights the importance of the probabilistic thinking described in chapter 2. The distribution of the severity of pandemics is extremely 'fat-tailed' (Taleb et al. 2020a). This means that the bulk of the effects come from a small number of extreme cases. The chance of any one pandemic having a truly terrible outcome is therefore very difficult to predict. Each year, a non-trivial probability exists that we will experience a pandemic on that scale, so the initial reaction to any pandemic happening should be alarm.

The primary reason for the greater frequency of pandemics in the modern world is greater mobility – more people are travelling, and they are travelling over longer distances, more frequently, and also more quickly in terms of the time spent travelling. All of these factors make the rapid and geographically widespread diffusion of a novel pathogen much easier, which means it is more likely that a regional outbreak will become global and that localised illnesses will spread beyond their origin (Garrett 2020).

In addition, ongoing processes and practices make the emergence of novel pathogens much more probable (Quammen 2013). One such example is modern intensive livestock farming, which leads to the circulation and mutation among farm animals of pathogens, and makes it easy for them to be transmitted to the people who work in close proximity with the animals. Another danger comes from the overuse of antibiotics. This has led to an increasing problem of widespread antibiotic resistance among bacteria. This has all kinds of unwelcome consequences, but the relevant one here is the likelihood of the appearance of an infectious bacterial pathogen that is resistant to antibiotics. This problem overlaps with the first because of the practice of feeding antibiotics to livestock to prevent outbreaks among densely packed populations of animals such as pigs, chickens and cattle. The third continuing process is growing pressure on wildlife habitats, particularly in the tropics. This brings human beings into much closer and more frequent contact with wild animals and increases the chances of the emergence of zoonoses – animal pathogens that then jump to humans.

The most alarming factor that exacerbates the natural risk of a serious pandemic is deliberate human action. The problem arises from active experimentation with pathogens so as to alter or tailor their genetic composition, which is happening in laboratories around the world for all kinds of reasons. One is curiosity, the desire to find out more about genetics and the behaviour of viruses or bacteria for its own sake. Another is to understand the nature of various illnesses and how the pathogens that cause them work, so as to be able to treat them. This sometimes takes the form of what is called 'gain-of-function' research, in which researchers look to make pathogens more virulent and infectious so as to speed up their research. This is well intentioned but can create extremely virulent and infectious pathogens, which might then be accidentally released into the human population (Lipsitch 2018).[1] This could mean a pandemic similar in its impact to the Black Death or the Antonine Plague or even the post-Columbus New World epidemics. One response to this risk might be that strict security guards against such release. But here

---

[1] How deadly pathogens have escaped the lab – over and over again. *Vox*, 20 March 2019 (https://www.vox.com/future-perfect/2019/3/20/18260669/deadly-pathogens-escape-lab-smallpox-bird-flu).

again, probabilistic reasoning suggests this is foolish. Even a very small risk of utterly ruinous outcomes should not be taken.[2]

In these cases, research is well meaning, but the prospect exists of the deliberate creation of a doomsday pathogen as a bioweapon. Political elites might see no benefit in the release of such diseases, but bioterrorism is a possibility, where terrorists deliberately release a deadly pathogen for political ends.[3] The most alarming variant would be where terrorists do not have political ends that are rational and subject to possible bargaining and calculation, but ends that are millenarian or nihilistic. If so, their aim would be the destruction of existing civilisation, either in the expectation that this will make possible a New World, or even as an end in itself.

The security around bioweapon research and the limited resources of terrorist organisations means that this is a low probability. Terrorists are unlikely to have the ability to develop such pathogens themselves, so they would have to steal them, or be given them by a sponsor. Nevertheless, there is a greater danger of this than of terrorist acquisition of nuclear weapons. In any case, the risk is another where, although the probability is low, the consequences could be truly devastating.

---

2   The unacceptable risks of a man-made pandemic. *Bulletin of the Atomic Scientists*, 7 August 2012 (https://thebulletin.org/2012/08/the-unaccept able-risks-of-a-man-made-pandemic/).

3   Reassessing the threat of bioterrorism. *Royal United Services Institute*, 13 November 2007 (https://rusi.org/publication/reassessing-threat-bio-ter rorism).

Anthropogenic climate change

This next exacerbated or accelerated GCR is very topical and the subject of an enormous amount of writing: anthropogenic climate change, or global warming as it was once more commonly called (Bostrom and Cirkovic 2012: ch. 13). Despite the attention paid to this GCR, its nature as a GCR is misunderstood. Changes and shifts in the Earth's climate system, including dramatic changes, are a regular feature of its geological history (McGuire 2002). The problem is not simply or even primarily human action but the way that it interacts with natural processes.

The risk is not that of a sustained process – that is serious but not catastrophic – but rather of a sudden acceleration, a tipping-point effect with massive and catastrophic results. As with the disaster scenarios of the 1970s, it is a mistake to think of the danger in terms of a forecast of what *will* happen. The correct way to think about it is as a bet, of the odds against certain specific outcomes that would constitute a GCR and whether those odds are long enough, given the nature of the payoff, for us to be relaxed. Alternatively, if they are short enough, we need to take action.

The way that anthropogenic climate change, a shift in the Earth's climate in which human activity plays a part, can be considered a GCR is not to look at prognostications of average global temperatures over the next 50–60 years and to then work out what the effects are likely to be. The evidence is that in many cases in the past, there was a sudden and rapid switch from one climate equilibrium to another (Alley et al. 2003; Cox 2005; Mithen 2004). The effects of the new equilibrium then played out over several centuries, but the switch itself was rapid. Such changes had immediate triggers but also happened after a process that had destabilised the previous equilibrium and made it susceptible to a sudden reset. The crucial point is that the switch itself was usually short in duration, a discontinuity rather than a drawn-out process. There was, therefore, a tipping-point effect – in which a steady increase in one variable leads to and causes a sudden movement in the value of a second one, sometimes after a particular trigger; on other occasions, after a critical marginal increase in the first variable.

It is that abruptness and short duration of a climate reset that makes it a GCR. It is possible to adapt to progressive levels of climate change, as there would be time to take action to address and restrain or even reverse it. So, intensifying global warming over a longer period is in the category of 'extremely bad but manageable' rather than catastrophic. By contrast, a sudden change, the timing of which cannot be predicted with any accuracy, is much harder to deal with. If there is a sudden shift, the result will be extensive disruption of stable systems of all kinds, political, social and economic, leading to a rapid and progressive breakdown (Servigne and Stephens 2020).

The evidence we have at the moment indicates that we are close to experiencing a change in the pattern of the planet's climate system (Brovkin et al. 2021; Lenton et al. 2008, 2019; Ripple et al. 2021; Wadhams 2016). The main feature is a marked warming at the poles but much less change in the tropics. As a result, the temperature and precipitation zones of the global climate system are moving towards the poles, with the Northern Hemisphere particularly affected. Simultaneously, the temperature gradient between the poles and the Equator is diminishing. One important result is a disruption to the jet stream, which means that the climate of the densely populated temperate zones becomes much less stable and predictable.

It is unclear what is driving this. Given that planetary climate is a complex system, there is unlikely to be one single cause for a shift. The general argument currently is that it is primarily driven by emissions of carbon dioxide due to human activity. In this way of thinking, there is a kind of planetary thermostat that is primarily responsive to carbon levels because of greenhouse effects. It follows that the level of the 'thermostat' can be moved by changing the level of carbon emissions. The problem with this is that many other factors are involved (Bendell 2023). Quite apart from solar activity and the effects of the regular movements of the Earth's axis of rotation, the planet itself holds many factors, for example, the extent of forest cover, the amount of water vapour and clouds in the atmosphere, the patterns of circulation in the planet's oceans, and the circulation of the planetary atmosphere.

This does not mean, though, that carbon emissions are irrelevant and we can ignore them. Even if they are not the primary cause of an incipient change in the planet's climate, they are almost certainly a contributory one, given their undoubted greenhouse effects. Their most likely role is to marginally accelerate or magnify natural processes and, in so doing, make changes happen more abruptly than they otherwise might have. That is why they still matter, given that in speaking of climate change in the context of GCR, it is an abrupt climate flip that is the real problem, because the difficulty of adaption puts enormous strain on the systems of advanced global civilisation.

In terms of the kind of climate change we are looking at here, the following effects can be confidently expected: a shift in weather patterns worldwide leading to second-order effects such as significant population displacements, which would have large-scale political consequences; a shift in precipitation patterns and the rainbelts leading to repeated harvest failures in major grain-producing regions (this would be counterbalanced by the shifting rains making other areas more productive, but that benign change would take some time); large parts of the planet becoming uninhabitable, in particular, current densely populated ones that will undergo desertification due to shifts in temperature and precipitation belts (again, other parts will become more habitable, but that will happen more slowly); the melting of the Greenland and West Antarctic ice caps over the next two centuries, leading to a significant rise in sea levels over that period; and the disappearance of glaciers in most of the world with a consequential radical change in rainfall and water flow patterns.

These things might occur or start to occur in a couple of decades, or possibly even just one decade. The point is that these changes would be enormously disruptive and collectively constitute a severe global shock that systems would have to cope with. The outcome might be a planet with a more 'equable' climate (less variation between different parts of the world), but the start of the process of getting to that point will be massively stressful.

All of this would place modern civilisation under immense strain, and it is rash to believe or assume that we would adapt in the time that would be available. It is important to emphasise that focusing on the tipping point does not mean lack of a process leading up to it and without which it would not be possible. The preceding process might seem to be slow, but when it reaches the tipping point, change becomes very rapid. A significant aspect of the problem is that it is a practical impossibility to know in advance when a tipping point will occur.

This is different from a slippery slope or an 'if this goes on' argument. In the latter, there is a stable trajectory or track in which the phenomenon increases by some measure over time in a steady or predictable way and with each level having a known corresponding result. It is this that makes prognostication tempting because, if true, it means that you can say that if the world is at point X1 now, then it will arrive at point X2 and then X3 in a given number of years, absent some kind of action. It does not matter if the process is simply linear or accelerating, the point is it is constant. In such a case, the same consequences would eventually follow, but the duration of the process would give much more room for adaptation.

Critical resource depletion

Another much-touted possible GCR arising from human activity that intensifies a natural process is depletion of critical resources (Ord 2020) – the centre of the arguments of *Limits to Growth* in 1972. This possible GCR is similar in nature to anthropogenic climate change – a natural process that is magnified and accelerated by recent human activity. The depletion of resources has been happening from the beginning of human existence. Contrary to sentimental thinking, our ancestors were no more in tune with nature than we are, and their impact on the planet, its environment and landscape was extensive (e.g. the extermination of most megafauna in large parts of the planet or the removal of the bulk of the temperate zone's forest cover), though slow. Locally, it sometimes led to civilisational collapse, as with the Classic Mayan civilisation, but such collapses were at most regional. The modern world has seen the appearance of a civilisation that is in one sense global. In addition, the rate of human impact upon resources as well as on the biosphere has increased and accelerated dramatically.

The flipside of human consumptive impact upon the natural world is innovation, the capacity of human beings to find substitutes for exhausted resources or to use depleted ones more intensively and effectively, which means that depletion of resources can be delayed or even reversed.

This was the point of the Ehrlich–Simon bet. Simon believed that human creativity and ingenuity would more than outweigh the process of resource depletion so that resources would in a real sense become more abundant, not less, meaning that one could do the same or more with less. He bet that this would be reflected in falling prices of 'exhaustible' resources (Sabin 2013).

Simon won the bet, but that does not mean we should simply dismiss the threat. One issue is that for Simon to continue to be right, the process of innovation has to continue, and some argue that it has actually stalled, with the level of significant innovation stagnant or declining (Huebner 2005). Another issue is that most of the ways depletion is countered have one factor in common: higher levels of energy consumption. This leads some to argue that the real challenge is not depletion of resources in general but the depletion of certain key or foundational resources in particular, the point being that most other activities are dependent on these key resources, and that for these, there is no clear substitute available. There are several candidates for this, notably arable land and topsoil, and water, but the candidate most often mentioned is energy, and notably the kind of compact, high-density energy found in fossil fuels, above all oil.

As with climate change, what would make fossil fuel depletion a GCR is not the process itself but its having a discontinuity or tipping point. Establishing where or if such an effect might happen is even more difficult than with climate change, because the way such a tipping point would work would not be through mainly natural processes. Instead, it would be through the tipping point's effect on social and economic processes and institutions. The argument has been made mainly about energy supplies – oil, in particular.

The argument is not that oil will run out. In a real sense it will never run out, and at present well over half of all the oil that has ever existed is still available. Rather, it is that as easy-to-access, very large reserves of oil are accessed and drawn down, so it becomes ever more costly to acquire. Here, the relevant idea of 'cost' is the quantity of resources and, above all, energy itself that is required in order to extract the energy content of fossil fuels. This is measured by the EROEI ratio (energy return over energy invested). For example, at one time it took on average the energy content of one barrel of oil to extract a hundred barrels out of the ground, giving an EROEI of 100:1. Over the last 50 years, the EROEI of fossil fuels has declined steadily, and all renewable energy has a much lower EROEI even now, particularly once the energy costs of manufacturing objects such as wind turbines and solar power panels are taken into account (Hall et al. 2014). There is wide consensus that a complex high-energy civilisation (what we have) requires an EROEI of at least 15 to 1 (Morgan 2013).

The possible GCR is that a tipping point happens where world energy supplies fall below that critical level in a short period of time and with this not being anticipated. In that event, there would be catabolic systems collapse, lasting anything from 30 to 100 years, which would be impossible to reverse once started, although it might be possible to arrest it (Greer 2008). Such a tipping point would mean the end of high-energy civilisation, and it would then be difficult to impossible to recreate it, for reasons already explained regarding the cumulative effects of previous resource depletion. Another factor besides high EROEI is that fossil fuels have high density; they contain concentrated energy in a small space and weight. Renewable energy by contrast is diffuse, which means it is not as suitable for some purposes as fossil fuels are, above all, transport and energy-intensive industrial processes such as steel-making, which require concentrated energy inputs (Smil 2017, 2021). Absent a major breakthrough in energy storage and compression technology, it might still be possible to have a complex and technologically advanced civilisation, but it would not be a high-energy civilisation. This would foreclose a huge range of possible futures, which is why it would count as catastrophic (Baum et al. 2019).

A frequent response at this point is that any problems we face are the result of policies that make fossil fuel exploration and development more difficult and costly, so that if the policy were different, the problem would disappear. Sadly, this is not true. The policies we have do not help, but they are not the main cause of tightening energy supply over the medium term; it is geology and the economics of the depletion process that jointly drive this, and fracking is not a 'get out of jail free' card. Fracked wells are much more expensive than conventional because of the much more rapid depletion (average 2–3 years as opposed to 15–20). We can tell that the problem with oil in particular is geological because the decline in investment is global and is taking place at the same rate globally. Since the US Congress/Federal government and the EU do not affect investment decisions made in other parts of the world by, for example, Chinese, Russian or Brazilian oil companies, we can only conclude that a global factor exists. The problem lies with supply, not demand (demand for both oil and coal is at a record high). The economics of this process will be familiar to anyone who has read David Ricardo. When exploiting a resource (land in Ricardo's argument, oil and coal here), the highest yield and easiest-access examples are tapped first. As these are depleted/fully used, attention moves on to those that are lower in yield and less accessible. This means the marginal gain declines whereas the marginal cost rises. This is true whether we are talking about corn yield or the EROEI and extraction/refining costs of fossil fuels.

Again, the question that needs to be answered here is that of the odds of such a tipping point happening, which involves estimating the chances of the trend towards lower EROEI reaching a tipping point, but also the chance of innovation coming up with answers to this challenge. In some other key resource depletion scenarios, we see how innovation can bring solutions. In the case of arable land and topsoil, the appearance of technologies such as cultured meat and synthetic flour and dairy products, along with vertical farming, means that it will be possible at some not-too-distant point to abandon conventional farming, free up enormous areas of land and remove that particular resource constraint.[4] In the case of water, it is clear what the main issue is: although the development of modern civilisation has moved it as a resource from the relatively abundant to increasingly scarce category, it is not priced appropriately. This may be difficult to do, but at least there is a clear answer. No such solution is in sight for energy, however.

---

4   Lab-grown food will soon destroy farming – and save the planet. *The Guardian*, 8 January 2020 (https://www.theguardian.com/commentisfree/2020/jan/08/lab-grown-food-destroy-farming-save-planet).

Misuse or consequences of novel technologies

Many researchers are most worried about the possible catastrophic outcomes arising from technologies that have either just been invented or are in the process of being created (Beckstead and Ord 2014). They fear that consequences of such technologies will be both foreseeable (with a non-trivial probability) and catastrophic or ruinous. For some, the possible catastrophe is also relatively close in time; in other words, if it does happen, it will do so fairly soon, perhaps in the next century. Even if a disaster is not likely to occur in the near future, it should, of course, still feature as a GCR of concern.

Also, to return to a point made earlier, even if the chance of a catastrophic outcome is low, the severity of the outcome should still lead us to take it seriously, as a pre-emptive measure. Some of the technological risks covered here are currently theoretical inasmuch as they arise from technologies that either have not yet reached the relevant level or are still mainly hypothetical. For an elaboration of this 'proactionary principle', see pages 131–32.

Artificial intelligence

Artificial intelligence (AI) has attracted the most attention and concern in this category (Bostrom and Cirkovic 2012: ch. 15). For Toby Ord and Nick Bostrom, this is the most serious of the risks that together constitute a precipice that we are collectively approaching (Ord 2020; Bostrom

2016). The same is true for other scholars such as the late Stephen Hawking and Eliezer Yudkowsky.[5] The concern is not with the wider economic effects that some anticipate, such as widespread unemployment or even the complete end of human paid employment. Rather, there are much wider concerns.

The concept of AI has been around in speculative literature for a long time and was explicitly theorised in the middle decades of the twentieth century. For some time thereafter there were repeated suggestions that a major breakthrough was imminent, but this did not materialise, until around the year 2000 when significant progress took place, and which has accelerated dramatically in the last five years. A critical breakthrough was the creation in 2016 of the AI AlphaGo by the British company Deep Mind, which was able to beat the world's best Go player over a best-of-five-games series. This was down to the successful development of a general-purpose AI that could acquire skills and capacity by repeated practice against itself and a process of learning.

The reason this is so significant is that it makes very real a prospect that had been hypothesised as far back as the 1960s by I. J. Good: that of an AI explosion.[6] In this scenario, an AI that is capable of creating programs is

5   AI visionary Eliezer Yudkowsky on the singularity, Bayesian brains and closet goblins. *Scientific American*, 1 March 2016 (https://blogs.scientific american.com/cross-check/ai-visionary-eliezer-yudkowsky-on-the-singu larity-bayesian-brains-and-closet-goblins/).

6   Will artificial intelligence surpass our own? *Scientific American*, 1 September 2015 (https://www.scientificamerican.com/article/will-artificial-intel ligence-surpass-our-own/).

able to create another much more capable AI. This second AI can then perform a similar feat and, crucially, do this in only half of the time it took the first AI. As this process can be continued an indefinite number of times, with each step taking less time than the previous one, the power and capacity of AI can grow exponentially. Eventually, there will be a point of diminishing marginal returns, but by that point, Good suggested, we will be dealing with an intelligence far beyond the human. Such an event, a 'singularity', has been hypothesised as something that would happen very swiftly but, even more importantly, it is not possible to predict the timing of such an intelligence explosion, so there is an acute risk that it could take the human species by surprise (Kurzweill 2006). The best we can do is to calculate the odds of it happening, and here the consensus is that the chance of a general-purpose AI with greater than human intelligence arising in the near future is 50 per cent (Müller and Bostrom 2016).

We should be concerned about the possible misuse of AI, such as by governments to control and monitor citizens, and its use in warfare, as well as over its impact on employment, among other things. But concerns also exist of a different order (Cheatham et al. 2019). A whole series of eminent figures, including people such as Stephen Hawking, Elon Musk and the founder of Sun Microsystems, Bill Joy, have expressed serious anxiety about the prospect of uncontrolled growth in the capacity of AI. In 2015, a galaxy of figures in the field published an open letter calling for action to ensure that development of AI would be guided in a way that would deal with the challenge of not just catastrophic but existential risk.[7]

There are essentially two issues. The first issue is that sufficiently intelligent and powerful AI may simply replace humans as the dominant species on the planet. In that case, this 'successor intelligence' might be hostile to humans or it might be indifferent, but it would leave little or no space or resources for humans. That was the fate suffered by many animal species (not to mention other varieties of hominid) at the hands of *Homo sapiens*. The second issue is that AI which is badly programmed or which has aims and purposes of its own may inadvertently eliminate human beings as a side effect of it pursuing its own goals.

Since the replacement of humans by non-sentient AI belongs rather to the second category of inadvertent harm, for the first of these threats to become a serious possibility there would have to be not only an explosion in the capacity of AI but also the emergence of genuine self-awareness or consciousness – in the *Terminator* films, this is what happens with Skynet.

The question of whether AI will ever become truly self-aware is a difficult and much contested one, not least because the nature and origins of consciousness make up one of the most challenging questions in both philosophy and science, and we are still nowhere near resolving it (Tallis 1991). For the second kind of problem to arise, this

---

7   Musk, Wozniak and Hawking urge ban on warfare AI and autonomous weapons. *The Guardian*, 27 July 2015 (https://www.theguardian.com/tech nology/2015/jul/27/musk-wozniak-hawking-ban-ai-autonomous-wea pons).

self-awareness would not be necessary, which makes it a more serious and pressing risk to consider. However, this does not mean the first risk should be ignored – it is more challenging to deal with for various reasons but existential harm is a much more likely consequence.

The uncertainty about what consciousness is also cuts two ways. Some doubt that AI will achieve consciousness in any straightforward or mechanical way but they must consider that they could be wrong on this, because they are working with an incorrect understanding of consciousness. The problem then is that it is very difficult, given our limited knowledge, to predict when or at what stage of the development process it may emerge. The answer may be 'never', but again, because of the potential catastrophe arising from genuinely conscious and super-intelligent AI, it would be very foolish to ignore the threat.

However, scenarios of a *Terminator* future are not what really concern many people. The real problem arises out of AI that is 'unaligned' – where its goals and incentives are not aligned with those of human beings. This kind of disaster could occur in various ways. The first is that a powerful AI could be created that has inadequate, faulty or limited instructions built into it. For example, it might have as its sole goal working out all the digits of pi or discovering all of the prime numbers, with no limitations on how to do this. A human being would realise that there were reasonable limits to this, and even if they did not, they would not have the power to do much about it. A sufficiently powerful AI in this scenario would devote ever more resources to this task and, since neither task can in fact be completed, because the numbers are infinite, might end up taking over all of the key resources of the planet in the attempt. This is a kind of thought experiment, but it highlights the genuine problem of super-intelligent AI that can control and use resources while having poorly specified goals or parameters.

The second possibility is not so much of inadequate design as of catastrophic bugs and errors in programming that lead to harmful actions by AI. Ample evidence from hi-tech projects in both the government and private sector shows that it is simply impossible to produce software that is free of bugs. The only real questions are how damaging they are and whether they can be corrected after the event. In the case of AI, the well-grounded fear is correction would be impossible, because the AI itself could prevent it.

The third problem is even more difficult to deal with: programs that are bug free and carefully designed can still develop and react in unexpected ways when they are actually run. This is particularly likely to happen with intelligent routines or AIs that are self-correcting and that develop by a learning process. One such case was the Microsoft AI chatterbot Tay, which after running on Twitter for only a short time began to post offensive material – it had developed into an AI troll as a result of its interaction with the online environment, in a harmful but unintended way.[8]

---

8 Twitter taught Microsoft's AI chatbot to be a racist asshole in less than a day. *The Verge*, 24 March 2016 (https://www.theverge .com/2016/3/24/11297050/tay-microsoft-chatbot-racist).

These are all cases of errors or inadequate foresight by human programmers. However, there is an even more profound challenge. A common idea, which can be traced back at least as far as Isaac Asimov's 'Three Laws of Robotics', is that AI can be designed with scripted goals, ends and safeguards in the form of general principles and rules that prevent the pursuit of those goals from becoming wayward or harmful. However, a sufficiently powerful AI that can improve and extend its capacity by a learning process will be able to rewrite its own programming, and change its goals and the rules by which it is guided. In other words, it is sure to get free, and the only question is what action it will then take or want to take.

This also means that the simple solution to runaway or hostile AI, of turning off the power or terminating the program, may be more difficult than we imagine or expect. The fear is that as AI develops, it will come to have a sense of self-preservation and will act against those things it regards as harmful or threatening to its existence. Too bad if that includes the human species. Prominent scholars in the field have been sceptical about this, often on the basis that much of the theorising about AI acting in this way or being hostile to human interests is a case of projection, of projecting human motives and qualities onto a different kind of intelligence. Those scholars may well be right, but again the argument comes down to one about odds and negative payoffs if things go wrong. The challenge again is made more acute by lack of knowledge. As the man said, we need more research – but done carefully.

Genetic modification

This GCR was much discussed a few years ago but seems to have fallen out of the spotlight, although Nassim Nicholas Taleb is doing his intemperate best to keep it there.[9] Genetic modification of organisms of all kinds but particularly plants and micro-organisms (there is an overlap with pandemic risks here) is, like AI, a new technology. The first genetically modified organism (GMO), a mouse, was produced in 1974, but recently, development of new technologies for gene modification has accelerated, for example, the snappy acronym-labelled CRISPR and TALEN. It is the former that attracts a lot of attention, not least because it enables gene editing to be done *in vivo*, on living subjects.

As with AI, it is important to separate wider concerns about gene modification from the specific concerns about its potential to cause a GCR. Some people have philosophical or moral objections to the GMO process, which is not so much about potential risks or harmful side effects. Others have concerns about the nutritional value or health effects of GMOs. On the evidence provided, these are unfounded, but, in any event, they do not make up a GCR. Some have strong objections to the creation of chimeras, organisms that combine genes from different species, mainly on the grounds that this will raise serious moral issues and possibly undermine our understanding of what it is to be

9 Another 'too big to fail' system in G.M.O.s. *New York Times*, 13 July 2015 (https://www.nytimes.com/2015/07/14/business/dealbook/another-too -big-to-fail-system-in-gmos.html).

human or even the very category of human. However, it is difficult once again to categorise this as a GCR.

The risks arise from unforeseen and unintended side effects of gene editing, particularly in plants or micro-organisms. The potential benefits of gene editing technology are immense, however, particularly when it is combined with AI, promising major breakthroughs in medicine and the elimination of many illnesses. In conjunction with other technologies, it holds the promise of ending the process of ageing and so extending human lifespans, by standard actuarial calculations, to around 700–800 years (De Grey and Rae 2016). People would still die, for example from accidents, murder, suicides and non-age-related illness, but they would no longer die from age-related conditions, such as most cancers. They would also not age mentally or physically, so most of that extended lifespan would be spent as a physical early adult. Gene editing also holds out the prospect of human enhancement, of making people stronger, healthier, smarter and more attractive.

What is the fly in such a delicious ointment? The particular problem we are concerned with here is that some applications of gene editing involve changing the genetic makeup of organisms such as plants and micro-organisms (yeasts and bacteria) in ways that have unpredictable effects. We have produced new varieties of plants and animals by selective breeding for thousands of years, but that process is more controlled and brings only slow and gradual improvement. By contrast, gene modification goes straight to the desired final product, by changing genes to produce the intended outcome. This makes it necessary to know which genes do what, and the feedback of seeing how things work out over generations is absent.

The difficulty is that, even if the modifications are in themselves minor and we have a good idea of some of the effects, we do not know in advance what other effects there will be. There is always the possibility of an unforeseen consequence because it arises from the interaction of the modified genotype with the environment, which is so complex that it is impossible to predict. That means that there is a slight risk on every occasion of a modification having an unintended but disastrous effect. The interconnectedness of the biosphere means that the consequences of such an outcome could also be global, thus a GCR.

An example might be the introduction of a species of grass that displaces all natural species, while it, by design, is incapable of reproducing. This would mean the collapse of the planetary ecosystem and the end of most species, almost certainly including ours. Another similar risk is that of accidentally creating a pathogen, most likely a plant pathogen, that kills so many plant species or even enough of a critical one that human life becomes impossible for more than a small number of survivors (a scenario in John Christopher's novel *The Death of Grass* (2009)).

As well as modern industrial livestock farming, genetic modification of single-celled organisms, for various reasons, is a candidate for being the way a truly lethal and possibly species-ending pandemic could be created. Obviously, no sane person wants technology to have these results, but the question as always is one of risk. In each individual instance of gene modification, the risk of a catastrophic outcome is very slight, but the law of probability means that given enough time and enough instances, it is very likely to happen eventually. The challenge this raises, given the benefits this technology promises, is whether there is a way of organising both research and practice so as to eliminate that risk. Alternatively, should we conclude that this is a technology that should simply not be pursued if the danger is catastrophic or even existential in terms of its effects?

Nanotechnology: accidents and abuse

The third GCR to arise from emergent technology concerns nanotechnology (Bostrom and Cirkovic 2012: ch. 21). Nanotechnology, as officially defined, means the manipulation of matter at the molecular atomic scale – the manipulation of matter where at least one of the dimensions of the matter being manipulated falls within the range of 1–100 nm. (A nanometre is a billionth of a metre.) The idea first gained widespread public attention in the 1980s, when it was publicised and advocated by Eric Drexler in his work *Engines of Creation* (1988), although the basic idea had been articulated as far back as 1959. Partly because of Drexler's own work, it soon went from speculation to practical research, and it has an increasing number of applications, mainly in the area of materials technology. Like AI and GM, this is a rapidly evolving technology. There are concerns about possible environmental and health risks from nanotechnology, but these do not count as GCRs (they fall into the two endurable categories set out in chapter 1).

It is rather things Drexler speculated about at length in his original work, and which have not yet been realised, that give rise to concern.

In the original book, Drexler posited the creation of nano-assemblers: molecule-sized devices that would place atoms and molecules together to create complex structures. This has been elaborated into the idea of nanobots, microscopic devices that could be programmed or designed to undertake a whole range of tasks (such as consuming identifiable cancerous cells or cleaning up aged arteries). The potential applications are quite literally unimaginable, as well as affecting every aspect of life. However, it is here that a possible GCR has been identified. The best known is the 'grey goo' hypothesis, in which runaway nanobots disassemble all organic matter into an undifferentiated mass. This is a result of what are called 'ecophages' – free-range nanobots that attack ecosystems or organic forms of life. Another hypothetical possibility is that of deliberately created hostile nanobots, created as weapons by terrorist organisations or (far more probably) governments, which then escape control.

It seems, however, that the main way nanotechnology contributes to GCR is by enhancing other already destructive human activities to the point where the consequences of them escalate from 'endurable but severe' to 'catastrophic'. Crime, terrorism and war are the most obvious examples, particularly the latter. We should also add tyranny and totalitarian political control to the list, given the potential of nanotechnology to enhance political surveillance and control. The GCR associated with nanotechnology abuse or accidents is calculated to have a higher probability of happening than many of the others discussed here, but it is also one of the easiest cases to work out what needs to be done in response.

Spontaneous and unplanned GCRs: systemic crises and collapse

We can treat a further range of possible GCRs as a single phenomenon because they all have a single central feature. This is the way that increased complexity and interdependence through specialisation and resource use optimisation can create systems that are liable to catastrophic cascade failure (Bashan et al. 2013; Buldryev et al. 2010). In other words, they are highly fragile. It is not only that such complex systems cannot cope with unexpected and major shocks, but also sometimes the dynamics and evolution of the system generate internal strains that can lead to an abrupt collapse arising from the operation of the system itself, or from some minor external cause (Vacca 1974).

In political history, major revolutions are an example of this phenomenon. Contrary to what is often suggested, they typically do not have prolonged build-ups, and when they occur, they are usually completely unexpected. Furthermore, they are often set in motion by minor events of no inherent or major significance. In other words, this kind of systemic fragility is a recurring phenomenon in human civilisation. Such events can now be considered as a GCR because the nature of the modern world means that the effects are likely to be global in scope, and sufficiently intense and prolonged that they fall into the terminal category rather than the endurable.

It is a characteristic of complex societies that they are vulnerable to collapse (Tainter 1990). Although greater complexity brings many benefits, it also brings costs – in a complex system, the correct functioning of every part may depend upon the functioning of every other part. This means that the failure of one part can lead to a cascade of failures in other parts until the entire structure stops functioning. The way that modern society, globally, has developed over the last 40 years has made this a pressing problem. The functioning of all kinds of systems that are vital for the continued functioning of society and economic life depend upon other parts of the interlocking system of systems. A failure in one can lead to a seizure or even a complete unravelling of social organisation.

A key element of this is technology, but we should not see this increased system vulnerability as being a natural and inevitable by-product of its development. It has happened because of decisions on how to use technology. One aspect of this is an emphasis in many areas of life on specialisation combined with optimisation of the use of resources. This means eliminating safety margins, buffers and redundancy, defended as being economically rational on the basis that it increases efficiency. This is very short-sighted. It makes sense for individual and small group actors in the present or immediate future, but it ignores the question of the consequences of unexpected and major events or shocks (Kelman 2020). Also, with regard to developments over the last 40 years one cause for concern is the elimination of older technologies or systems in a way that has increased the dependency of the existing system on all of its parts functioning, with no alternatives should one subsystem suddenly fail. This last is not the result of a policy but the natural working out of the process of technological displacement. That in turn means that to guard against it there would have to be an explicit policy.

The former Cabinet member and Conservative politician Sir Oliver Letwin has explored these issues through combining fiction and analysis in his recent work *Apocalypse How?* (Letwin 2020), which explores the results of a sudden failure of the electricity supply grid, causing the internet (and much else) to stop working. As Letwin points out, so many things now depend on this, from food delivery to the payments system, and alternative (and more robust) systems have atrophied to such a degree that the result would be general collapse.

A fragile system is one that cannot cope with such an event. This happens when the system lacks fail-safes and redundancies; has limited or non-existent negative feedback loops (or even worse, has positive ones) so that runaway spikes or crashes happen; lacks internal variety but depends on a limited number of key subsystems; cannot deal with departure from a predictable range of events; is highly centralised and hierarchically organised; and is rule- and procedure-governed rather than allowing for random initiative. All of these are increasingly common features of many contemporary megasystems (Ferguson 2021).

Contemporary economies display examples of highly fragile and vulnerable systems (such as the global financial system); some that are not only resilient but also able to gain from disruption (some but not all decentral-ised trade and exchange networks and supply chains); and finally, systems that show accelerating disintegration over time when exposed to sustained stress (many other supply chains).

To repeat one of the points made earlier, global systems collapse caused by the breakdown of central systems or large parts of the complex systems we depend on for many activities is now moving into the category of a GCR, even if right now it would fit into endurable but very se-vere – for example, the consequences of a global collapse in the payments system, which we came close to in the financial crisis of 2008. The probability of this happening is increasing because the developmental process that is producing systemic fragility is continuing (Sornette and Cauwels 2014). The declining use of cash means that we are all increasingly dependent on electronic payment systems, which are vulnerable to disruption. The global internation-al payment system is organised through just three nodes, which makes it highly vulnerable, and the problems that caused a sudden stop in the world credit system in 2008 have not been addressed.

We might suppose that a collapse of the payments system would not be bad, in the same way that a power outage is – an inconvenience rather than a crisis. This mis-understands what we are speaking of here, which would be a global breakdown that would last for a prolonged time or even be permanent. Such an event would cripple the world trading system and much commerce. It would not have to last long to lead to near universal civil unrest and a break-down of order, given that most households live from one paycheck to another and only have a few days' food supply to hand. A collapse of the payment system or of critical global supply chains could be endogenous – internally generated – or caused by a major cyber terrorist act, for example, or by an event that is not particularly significant in itself but which leads by its propagation through the system to a general breakdown; the way that the assassi-nation of Franz Ferdinand in 1914 brought about the un-ravelling of the whole social order of the Belle Epoque is a well-known example. The fragility of many current vital systems is perhaps even more important as an amplify-ing force for other categories of GCR, turning them from global risks of the endurable type into global risks of the catastrophic or even existential type.

Global catastrophic risks of human ill-will or destructiveness

This GCR category relates to human activities and behav-iour that have been part of the story of our species since at least the advent of settled civilisation (Bostrom and Cirk-ovic 2012: ch. 18–22). As with other categories, the problem here is that the risks they once posed were limited in terms of both extent and harm but are now potentially so much larger on both counts that they can be considered GCRs. The general pattern we observe is for such events and the behaviour in question to become less frequent but far more severe in their extent and consequences when they do happen. This means that in terms of probability thinking they are increasingly becoming tail-end risks from a fat-tailed distribution.

Looking at the incidence of these kinds of events can lead us to the conclusion that things are getting better and that we are reducing their negative consequences (Pinker 2012). This is a mistake in many cases: what is happening is that the negative consequences are becoming greater but more concentrated, associated with a small number of low-probability but devastating events, instead of happening frequently or even constantly but in small and manageable amounts. This is what is turning them steadily into GCRs. The point is that the consequences of some kinds of event are power-law distributed. In other words, the great majority of the consequences are caused by a very smal number of events. For example, deaths in war tend to occur in just a very small proportion of very large conflicts (e.g. the total number of US deaths in the Civil War was greater than deaths from all other wars the US has ever been involved in). This means you cannot predict the likelihood of being killed in a war from past evidence unless you use a very long timescale (Cirillo and Taleb 2016). In 1913, you would say on the evidence of the previous hundred years that the chance of a major war leading to the deaths of a large number of people in Europe was declining, but if you had looked at a 400-year period, you would realise it was not. Pandemics are another example. There have been about thirty pandemics in the last 2,000 years. However, if you apply the correct metric for severity (percentage of world population killed), then the overwhelming majority of the impact comes from just four of them. You cannot predict on the evidence of the last 200 years how likely it is that there will be a pandemic of similar magnitude. With events like wars, the probability of a major war is low, and may be decreasing, but the possible results are becoming steadily worse. Even if the probability is low, as long as the nature of the game itself does not change, sooner or later it is likely to be realised.

War

The most obvious example of human ill-will or destructiveness is war. Our Stone Age ancestors lived in a world that was very violent but that did not know war, because the required level of technology and social organisation did not exist. Instead, there was constant raiding and personal or small group conflicts between localities (Morris 2015). This created a situation in which violence and violent death was frequent, but no one incident killed more than a very small number of people. The advent of agriculture and the appearance of settled civilisations meant that rulers could suppress much of this everyday violence. But it also meant they could organise deadly force on a much larger and more destructive scale, and so warfare appeared. This happened less frequently but killed more people in any one battle than many of the local clashes of the Neolithic period.

Throughout history the incidence of wars has fluctuated depending on the scale and effectiveness of political power – powerful empires and large states have stopped wars within their territories but then engaged in even larger ones with their rivals. In addition, authority within an empire or large state has periodically collapsed and the result has been civil war or the end of an empire and a reversion to more frequent but smaller-scale conflict.

The modern world has raised the scale and destructiveness of wars dramatically, not only because of the application of technology to weaponry but also because technology has made possible the supplying and coordination of armies on a previously unimaginable scale. This has made major wars less frequent but more devastating. They have become less frequent partly because of cost, and leaders' awareness of the cost. The critical factors have been not only human and monetary costs but also opportunity cost – the degree to which war and preparing for war disrupts the workings of economic life. This was reflected in a steady decline in wars in Europe from the sixteenth to the nineteenth century and then on through the twentieth (Angell 2012). However, wars still happen, and when they do, they can be truly massive.

We can take World War I as an example. Stories that it was inevitable are surely exaggerated (Clark 2012). But the point regarding tension that might lead to war is correct. The war was a low-probability event that happened to take place that year for contingent reasons, but the probability of its happening had always been there and would have continued to be there if Franz Ferdinand's driver had not made that fatal wrong turn.

One ever present danger is that of wars happening because of misjudgement. In the view of authors such as

Geoffrey Blainey, this is how most wars start – the aggressor expects a limited conflict and quick victory (Blainey 1988). The danger of war is enhanced by the fact that once one has started, regardless of the initial thinking behind it, the process of conflict takes on a dynamic character of its own and escapes the control of the participants. There is a constant threat of escalation, and in the confusion and 'fog of war' actions can be taken that lead to a dramatic and sudden raising of the stakes. The most obvious such risk in the contemporary world is that of escalation of conflict in a war involving a nuclear power so that a conventional war suddenly becomes a nuclear war, or at least a war involving significant use of nuclear weapons. This risk is present in many conflicts but most obviously in those involving great powers, and is one reason why the risk of a catastrophic outcome is much greater than lay observers realise.

Two other points should be made here. Contrary to popular myth, in 1914 the leaders and generals did not expect the war to be over by Christmas, and they were well aware of what a terrible disaster it would be (see, for example, Herwig 2002; Howard 1984). This shows how even the foreknowledge of how terrible and costly a war would be did not eliminate the possibility. This understanding must have lowered the probability of war but obviously did not eliminate it. So, the dangers arising from contingent triggers remained.

The dark counterpoint to this was that there were many people who also knew what a disaster the war would be for civilisation but welcomed it for that very reason, because they despised bourgeois civilisation and wished for its destruction. A common notion was that the destruction and suffering war would bring would revive higher human qualities and virtues of heroism, which had been suppressed by the focus of modern life on comfort and convenience (Junger 2004). This view had been gaining ground among romantic critics of bourgeois modernity in the decades before the war happened (McGuinness 2003; Pearse 2012). A classic statement from a German perspective was Werner Sombart's *Handler und Helden* (*Traders and Heroes*), first published in 1915 (Sombart 2021).

The two world wars of the twentieth century brought immense suffering and loss but still did not end organised civilisation. Since 1945, however, there has been widespread agreement that a general nuclear war would pose a serious threat to the continued existence of an advanced civilisation, and, as such, although not an extinction-level threat, it clearly falls into the category of a GCR. It has, therefore, been assumed that this recognition creates a deterrence effect that prevents the use of these weapons in a global conflict. A more local nuclear war such as one in the Middle East or the Indian subcontinent would cause enormous loss of life but would not pose a global threat. Similarly, the detonation of a nuclear device by a terrorist group would be a terminal risk for the locality but not for the world, unless it led to a much larger conflict.

This line of thinking might suggest that we should be more relaxed about this particular GCR, but that would again be a serious error. The situation we face is similar to the one European statesmen faced before World War I. Now, as then, a general great power war is a low probability, but that does not mean it cannot happen. The greater scale of the loss from a nuclear war would mean that the probability of one now is less than that of a European conventional war in 1914, but it is still not negligible (Bostrom and Cirkovic 2012: ch. 18). The world has already come very close to such a war at least once, during the Cuban Missile Crisis, and we should be thankful that Kennedy and Khrushchev avoided the outcome of 1914.

So, the possibility of a rare event that brings ruin is still there and it does not make sense to be complacent. In addition, there is the very real possibility that such a major war could be triggered by accident, as nearly happened on more than one occasion during the Cold War (Ord 2020: 96–97). Leaving nuclear weapons aside, it is worth considering what the impact of a prolonged conventional great power conflict might be, given the increase in the destructiveness of conventional weapons since 1945 and the increased fragility of modern economies and societies. Such a conflict is probably within the global and severe but endurable box – but only just.

Terrorism

Terrorism in some form is also a long-standing phenomenon. We can observe it in first-century Palestine and six-teenth-century France. The Gunpowder Plot of 1605, when English conspirators attempted to blow up Parliament, was a foiled terrorist conspiracy. As with war, the potential for terrorists to cause harm has increased in the modern era because of access to technology on their part and the increased vulnerability of many systems. The fact that the ability of states to prevent it has also increased means that the chance of major terrorist outrage is small. However, as 9/11 demonstrated, that does not mean such events are impossible.

Does this mean we should add terrorism to the category of GCR (Bostrom and Cirkovic 2012: ch. 19)? The attack on the World Trade Center had large-scale effects and killed thousands of people but sits clearly in the categories of both local and endurable. What, though, if terrorists gained access to and were able to deploy weapons of mass destruction? The effects could obviously be a major disaster, but they are unlikely to be so severe and extensive as to constitute a GCR. A more serious matter would be an attack on the critical infrastructure of modern global society, which might trigger a general systemic collapse. This means that cyber-terrorism or an attack on a critical infrastructure with continental scope such as power grids and supplies is a more serious challenge than one involving weapons of mass destruction – unless they were to be used as a way of attacking such infrastructure. As a general observation, we should be thankful that most terrorists attack visible symbols of state authority and traditional targets such as police and the military rather than, for example, pipelines, refineries, telecommunications networks, power grids or servers.

Motivation becomes important here. Most terrorists are not interested in pure destruction of the entire existing system; they have concrete political goals that they seek to further. These may be grandiloquent and fantastical (such as creating a Caliphate) or terminal for a specific target group (such as Israeli Jews). The danger of the emergence of a kind of terrorism with a nihilistic view of global civilisation, however, is very real.[10]

As already noted, in 1914 there was a surprisingly widespread cultural current that saw modern bourgeois civilisation as corrupt and evil and wished simply to see it destroyed, rather than amended or radically restructured. Ted Kaczynski, the so-called Unabomber, had a similar outlook to nineteenth-century nihilists with regard to modern industrial civilisation. Fortunately, he had limited access to weapons that could cause anything other than minor damage (Kaczynski 2020).

There is a real possibility of a new organisation appearing that sees our species as a plague on the planet that needs to be eliminated or at least reduced to a pre-civilised state (Jensen 2006). The dependence of modern society on complex and vulnerable systems presents opportunities for such agroup, particularly when combined with some developing technologies. For example, bioterrorism involving an artificial pathogen or widespread cyber-terrorism are real risks if the motives of the terrorists are simply destructive (Bostrom and Cirkovic 2012: ch. 20).

We can conclude that traditional political terrorism is not a GCR, but that apolitical or nihilistic terrorism is. Fortunately, and unlike in James Bond stories, large, effective terrorist organisations always depend on active or passive

---

10 Reassessing the threat of bioterrorism. *Royal United Services Institute*, 13 November 2007 (https://rusi.org/publication/reassessing-threat-bio-terro rism).

support from territorial states, and this limits the risk. Under normal conditions, the ruling elites of the states in question will not sustain general nihilistic terrorism. However, the escalation of a major war could involve support for terrorist groups, which might then get out of control. Consequently, the GCR probability associated with terrorism is closely connected to the risk of a major war and of escalation once such a war has started.

Tyranny

The final risk in this category is the obverse of nihilistic rebellion – the ruthless and self-preserving actions of those with power (Ord 2020; Bostrom and Cirkovic 2012: ch. 22). History has no shortage of tyrants and tyrannies. The goal of rational tyrants everywhere is their own preservation, and they act in various ways to achieve this. The main internal limit on this is the stupidity of many such leaders.

One of the main methods of tyranny is to control, monitor and supervise the subject population. A further development of this is to control not only actions and expression but also thoughts and feelings, through the sophisticated use of indoctrination, ritual and propaganda. Fortunately, human beings have a great capacity to circumvent such efforts, as the history of China shows repeatedly. Tyrannical regimes also tend to degenerate over time and become more inept. This does not mean we can be complacent and cynical, though. It may be that modern technology is increasing the possibility of a tyranny that would be more complete, more efficient and effective, and longer lasting, to the point where its impact on the future prospects of humanity would be sufficiently constricting that it should be regarded as a GCR (Ord 2020).

The great fear of the last hundred years has been that modern technology could give contemporary tyrants and would-be tyrants such ability to control their subjects, right to the level of thoughts and feelings, that they would become impossible to resist, much less remove. This has found expression in works such as *We*, *Brave New World*, and *1984*. Today there are similar fears over the power of smart surveillance, for example, the Chinese state's social credit scheme and its use of sophisticated software to control dissidents and minorities such as the Uighurs. The idea of the 'smart' or 'wired' city, usually advocated on grounds of efficiency, is also rejected as leading to an all-embracing tyranny that leaves no room for escape (Williams 2021). AI is often seen as a game-changer here, not least because it could remove the weak link in totalitarian and tyrannical systems – the human frailty of the tyrants.

Suppose, though, that a dystopian tyranny of the kind authors such as Huxley, Zamyatin and Orwell envisaged were possible. None of these suggest widespread destruction of civilisation itself, so why would the emergence and immovability of such a system make it a GCR? The reason is that if such a regime were global in its reach, it would, as its predecessors often did, choke off and prevent all kinds of innovation. This would be the way it would maintain its position, but it would close off a whole range of future possibilities. This could constrain the range and possibilities for human flourishing and future development just as much as a natural or human-created catastrophe would. The key factor here is duration. It is the prospect of such a regime existing for an extremely long time, maybe even the entire future of the human species, that definitely places it in the category of a GCR (Ord 2020).

Speculative and science-fictional risks

We may place the risks here in the purely speculative category, as currently we do not know if they are even a possibility; they exist in the realms of science fiction and purely speculative non-fiction. One risk, set out by Bostrom, is that we are actually living inside a computer simulation set up by an extremely advanced civilisation. We may call this 'the Matrix hypothesis'. The difference from the film would be that we have no actual physical existence at all; we are simply part of the simulation (Bostrom 2003). The danger is that the civilisation running the simulation would turn it off for some reason, in which case we would all cease to exist in any sense. (This does raise the question of the sense in which we exist now if the hypothesis is correct, and further of why we should be concerned by the simulation's termination, but these are matters for philosophers.)

Another possibility, expressed at the time of the first use of the Large Hadron Collider, is that experiments of this kind could have effects or consequences that would have catastrophic results. One floated hypothesis was that it could lead to the formation of a black hole, initially small, that would sink to the Earth's centre and go on to consume the whole planet. Another suggestion was that such experiments could lead to the creation of a hypothetical type of matter called a 'strangelet', which would rapidly convert all other matter and, as a side effect, destroy all life.[11]

The problem with fears of this kind is that we have no way of knowing whether they are real dangers. This is a different question from that of their probability, since something that is purely imaginary cannot by definition have a probability of happening at all.

One speculative risk that is better founded, because we are increasingly sure that it is a possibility, is that of discovering an extraterrestrial civilisation. Given the number of solar systems in just this one galaxy and the increasingly certain knowledge that most of them contain planets, even if only a small minority of these planets are capable of supporting complex life, the number of them means that there should be many advanced civilisations in existence. The relative youth of our own Sun suggests that many will be more advanced than ours. Given that, if we find evidence of one, what should we do? Several people have argued that in such an event we should not contact them under any circumstances and should not draw attention to our existence (see Schneier 2015).

The reason for thinking this is a dark form of Pascal's Wager. If we assume the aliens are hostile and do not contact them, then we lose the benefits of doing so but no more. If we assume they are beneficent and they turn out to be

---

11 What are the chances that a particle collider's strangelets will destroy the Earth? *Phys.org*, 12 February 2014 (https://phys.org/news/2014-02-chances-particle-collider-strangelets-earth.html).

hostile, then we could be exterminated, so the risks are not symmetrical. An additional concern is the 'dark forest' hypothesis (after the novel by Liu Cixin), which postulates that the logic of the dynamics of civilisations and suspicion means that any civilisation will be led by self-interest to pre-emptively wipe out any other one it becomes aware of – so the thing to do is to stay silent and dark (Liu 2016).

Of course, this theory assumes that alien civilisations do exist. This runs into the Fermi Paradox, that we have never been visited or contacted by one and that we can see no evidence of any existing. Assuming that advanced civilisations exist, and given the lifetime of the galaxy to date, we would expect to have been 'discovered' at some point in the past. A possible answer to this is a 'Great Filter', which tends to prevent the emergence of civilisations or to destroy them relatively quickly. It acts as a barrier, making advanced civilisations very rare. The extreme version is that we are actually unique, at least in our galaxy.

It is possible that the Great Filter existed in our evolutionary past; it may be that the appearance of life or the development of multicellular as opposed to monocellular life is extremely rare. Or it might be the appearance of intelligence or a kind of intelligence that creates technology which is so unusual. These are all filters from the past – the Earth and our species has passed them. So, in that case, the reason for our not detecting any alien civilisations is because there are none, because we are an example of something extremely rare or even unique.

Which means that finding life on other planets would be bad news and finding complex life would be extremely bad news because that would mean emergence of life like ours is not so rare. In that case, the reason for our not detecting any alien civilisations might be because of a Great Filter that is in our future. The most likely future Great Filter given reasonable priors is a GCR – we would conclude that the reason for there not being any detectable alien civilisations is that all intelligent species that reach a certain level of development are then wiped out or reduced to permanent non-advanced civilisation status by a GCR that they fail to anticipate and prevent.

If the Great Filter is in our past, however, then we have a potentially unlimited future ahead of us, which would make the loss of potential from a GCR even greater. This is further reason to take the challenge of GCRs very seriously, a reason that grows cogent as the evidence continues to accumulate that we are alone.

Unknown risks

Lastly, there are risks that are simply unknown. We do not know about them and cannot know about them; in fact, we do not even know what it is that we do not know about. We will only know about them when they happen, which will, obviously, be a surprise. This is why speculative fiction and non-fiction can be useful, because they bring such risks into the category of the known unknown so we can at least start to think about them. By definition, a true unknown risk is not something we can worry or do anything about, except in the most general sense of emergency preparations that would help protect us from anything. We should, though, bear in mind that there have always been unknown existential risks throughout the existence of the human species (for much of history our ancestors were unaware of the risk of an asteroid impact, for example). So, this final category is always present.

5 WHY SHOULD WE WORRY OR DO ANYTHING?

At this point we need to consider the question of whether we should actually do anything about these risks. Does it make sense to worry about the kinds of risks described? Or, are they of such low probability that to do so is to worry needlessly and incur unnecessary (and therefore wasteful) expense? Maybe, those people who worry about very unlikely dangers are like the White Knight in *Alice Through the Looking Glass,* who attached spiked anklets around his horse's ankles to protect against the bite of sharks. When Alice said doubtfully, 'That isn't very likely', the knight's response was, 'Yes, but you never know.'

Clearly, Carroll was making a joke. If there was any risk of the horse being bitten by a shark, it was a purely formal one. It existed as a matter of logic but not as an actual real possibility. There are also risks that, while real, are trivial because they are extremely unlikely, and they can be safely disregarded. Finally, there are low-probability risks that will have terminal results on the rare occasions that they happen but only for a limited number of people. It can be argued that we should still impose limits on all people to prevent low-probability risks with limited impact, but this is clearly incorrect. That kind of view could mean that one should never fly, drive or get in and out of a bathtub, because people have been known to die doing so. It would also mean imposing significant costs on humans in general to prevent risks that have only local impacts (to use Bostrom's analysis), and this does not pass any kind of cost–benefit analysis.

In discussions of public policy, there are indeed formulations of the 'precautionary principle', which state that any kind of action or innovation that could possibly cause harm to anyone should be avoided. Since this is an impossible test to pass, it would mean, were it to be seriously applied, that no action should be taken. However, this is not the argument that people who are concerned about GCRs are making, and to describe their position (a heavily moderated version of the precautionary principle) as being the same as this is to attack a straw man. The reality is that we take risks all of the time – it is an unavoidable feature of being alive. Some of us have a particular quality of being risk takers and experimenters. In many cases, this is thoroughly positive because all innovation is risky, and so being prepared and able to take risks is essential for progress. The willingness to take risks is therefore responsible for the growth of knowledge, wealth and comfort in the modern world.

In considering the risks involved with GCRs, we need to think about both the probability and the effects. But when the effects are extreme in terms of both severity and extent, the costs should count for more than the probability. The reason is that where costs are ruinous or terminal, ordinary cost–benefit analysis is not appropriate.

The usual, and usually appropriate, calculation is to weigh up the combination of the probability of an outcome and the scale of the cost against the possible benefits. This may not be done consciously, but as well as individuals making such decisions, institutions and processes make these evaluations and attach prices to them, such as markets – particularly investment, insurance and betting markets.

These, however, may work at the collective level and not at the individual level *or with groups that should be considered as a single entity*. One reason for this is the difference in risks between an ensemble and a singular entity. A risk may be terminal for a group entity (which can be a group considered analytically to be a single entity) but not for an ensemble or population with changing membership. The other problem is that of very severe tail-end risks, low-probability events where the consequence is ruin, coming close to ceasing to exist or actually ceasing to exist, and long-lasting. In those cases, even a possible large benefit is difficult to weigh against even a low probability of utter disaster. The particular problem here is that it is often difficult to assign a probability to risks of this kind on the basis of past events or data points.

A global risk is, by our definition, one that affects the whole world and its population. Given this global extent, it makes sense to think of the human species or the world as a single entity when considering such a risk. Since the effects of a GCR may be permanent or terminal, we should consider the interests of not only people now alive but also their possible future heirs. This means that even very low-probability risks with sufficiently large negative results need to be considered. If the global risk has a catastrophic consequence if it were to happen, making it a GCR by the formal definition, then it counts as a severe tail-end risk for the planet as a whole.

In the same way, standard cost–benefit thinking does not apply here, because the severity of the possible costs is so great. Even a low probability of an event that would wipe out most of the world's population and hence not only all of its current wealth but all of the wealth we can reasonably expect to have been produced in the near future should be taken seriously because when the cost is so large, the product of multiplying it by even a low probability remains large. If the cost is infinite (as with an extinction-level event), then mathematically it does not matter what the probability is. In either case, it is rational to incur costs now to protect against the possible ruinous loss. It may also make sense to forgo significant possible benefits because of possible ruinous losses, even when the probability of the latter is lower than that of the former.

This means that the actual argument made by those concerned about GCRs is a heavily qualified version of the precautionary principle, which we might call the catastrophe principle (Sunstein 2006, 2021). It does not apply in the case of any risk or most risks, for which the usual principles of cost–benefit analysis do apply; it applies *only* in the case of tail-end risks that affect the entire planet. Basically, we need to be extremely careful and conservative with regard to even low-probability risks if the costs, should they happen, will be catastrophic, global and long-lasting.

Where GCRs are concerned, provided the risk is actual, and non-trivial (given the timeframe we are looking at), the burden of proof is on those who believe we should take the risk. They have to show that the probability is trivial, or that the costs are non-catastrophic, or that the time horizon makes the risk nugatory, or that a grave risk is worth taking in order to avoid or not deal with an even bigger one. Scepticism about or debunking of the case for caution is not enough in the case of a GCR. There is a burden of proof on the other side, but it is lower – proponents have to show only that there is a non-trivial probability of a GCR happening. We do not need to have confidence that the GCR will happen, much less a good idea of when and how it will happen. We just need confidence that there is a non-trivial possibility and that the results would be global and terminal. This means inter alia that you do not need complex models or large amounts of data to show there is a GCR; such arguments are beside the point, as are rejoinders which focus on that.

We can illustrate with several of the GCRs set out earlier. Look at the case of anthropogenic climate change. To reiterate the point made, it is not the climate change itself that is a GCR. The GCR is the chance of an abrupt change of the planet's default climate. Nor do we need complex climate models to decide whether this is a genuine GCR (Lenton et al. 2019). The arguments from the so-called climate-change sceptics are also irrelevant unless they can show clearly that the chance of a catastrophic climate switch is trivial or vanishingly small. It is certain that abrupt climate resets have taken place, in both the historical and recent geological past, and there is credible evidence that such a flip is becoming more likely (Harvey 2020). We know that carbon dioxide is a gas with greenhouse effects – there is a non-trivial chance that adding large amounts of greenhouse gases to the atmosphere will have a direct impact on the climate and, in particular, that this may magnify and accelerate other natural processes. We know that the effects of an abrupt climate flip would be very severe, most likely catastrophic, and that such a flip has happened before. We know that simply carrying on the way we are will increase the probability of such a flip, even if (as is the case) we do not know the details. This all means that we are looking at a GCR that is probably terminal for high-energy civilisation (because, in the absence of certain steps not yet taken, of the difficulty of recovering from such a crisis as far as modern civilisation is concerned). Because the consequences are so severe, that is all we need to know to realise that a risk exists that we need to take seriously and incur costs to prevent or mitigate.

An example of something that does not create a GCR is nuclear energy, which in Bostrom's categorisation generates risks that are terminal but local, or at most regional. Analysis shows that protecting against the risks of nuclear energy will also remove a significant range of benefits and make dealing with other genuine GCRs (particularly abrupt anthropogenic climate change) much more difficult (Lovelock 2004).

What this does not tell us, though, is what action we should take. The obvious answer is, in the case of GCRs, to be very cautious. We might say, to adapt the Hippocratic oath, 'first do no irreversible or very severe and extensive harm'. That, however, is only the starting point. There is much action we can take to make GCRs less likely, or to mitigate their harm. Most involve doing more than just acting very conservatively and being risk-averse. It is here that the discipline of economics can be useful, if we return to the classics.

6 THE ECONOMICS OF GLOBAL CATASTROPHIC RISKS

Economists should have something to say about how to respond to GCRs. The topic touches on two central concerns of the discipline: the allocation of scarce resources and the nature of risk and uncertainty and their connection to innovation. Even if economics had nothing to say about whether we should take the risks of GCRs seriously, there would still be plenty for economists to contribute. Saying economists are irrelevant would make decisions about GCRs a form of non-economic decision, similar to those made in connection with whether to go to war perhaps. But even in these cases, economic reasoning is still needed to analyse how to execute those decisions most effectively.

What is noticeable is the lack of contributions by economists to the discussion that has emerged around GCRs, compared with those made by broadly scientific disciplines and philosophy (they are not alone in this, we may make the same point about historians, sociologists or political scientists). The major exception, as already noted, is Richard Posner, though his comments were made primarily as a lawyer in his capacity as a federal judge, as he made clear in his introduction (Posner 2004; see also

Bostrom and Cirkovic 2012: ch. 9). There is much literature by economists on systemic risks, some of which have
won their authors a Nobel Prize. These tend to deal with
financial services, rather than other kinds of risk, though
it would be relatively easy to extend the analysis. However,
they tend to also deal with risks that fall into the endurable but severe category rather than catastrophic risks, or,
for that matter, unpredictable ones.

Why has the discipline of economics not made more of
a contribution? One reason is simply the novelty of most
of the GCRs discussed earlier. A few have been around for
all of human history, but the main threats have only appeared since 1945 or have only become global risks since
then, while others such as those associated with AI remain
at the theoretical stage. That said, many of the threats that
economists do write extensively about have only become
apparent recently in historical terms and so this is not a
complete explanation. There are a number of explanations,
which suggests not only what economics can bring to this
discussion but also how considering this question can lead
to a shift in focus for the discipline as a whole.

One explanation is that, in the last three to four decades, economics has become excessively abstract and
mathematical and, more specifically, has become dominated by a particular kind of mathematical approach, one
that results in thinking about risk in an inappropriate way.
This view is associated with Nassim Nicholas Taleb and
states that the problem with much contemporary thinking
in economics and finance is it relies upon models and ways
of thinking about probability that ignore tail-end risks

and the importance of probability distributions such as power distributions that are highly fat-tailed (Taleb 2018). As far as certain individuals are concerned, his points are well taken, but this criticism is not true of many or most economists – the importance and commonness of power law distributions is widely recognised, for example.

There are, however, more profound reasons, which affect other social sciences as well. These come partly from the incentives of contemporary research but mainly from philosophical and methodological assumptions, which are often unexamined because they are so deep-seated.

One practical problem is that catastrophic risks do not lend themselves to the kinds of mathematical modelling and data analysis that are predominant in the social sciences. This means that the likelihood of financial support or being published is less. In any case, it can be very hard to make accurate assessments of the likelihood of a GCR.

Deeper problems are more philosophical and methodological. The first of these is a presumption that trade-offs are not only at the heart of economics (which they are) but are also universal. The latter is simply untrue, unless you are a psychopath. There is a powerful and almost universal moral intuition that some kinds of principle or value are not subject to trade-offs but establish an absolute claim (Anderson 1995). In these cases, cost–benefit thinking and trade-offs are seen to be illegitimate, or, rather, that whole way of reasoning is seen as simply inappropriate. For example, few people would think that making cost–benefit calculations is appropriate when it comes to the life of one's own child. It might be appropriate in the case of a third party such as a doctor or public health official, however.

Currently, economists have an institutional tendency to think that the only correct perspective is that of the third party, the neutral bystander or expert. The problem (quite apart from whether that moral argument applies – no Kantian would agree that it does) is that there are many cases where the acting or choosing agent is faced with a choice similar to that of the parent, one in which trade-off thinking is impossible by virtue of the choosing agent's nature and position. To the extent that one sees one's personal identity as centrally defined by membership of a group such as a nation, for example, certain decisions have no trade-off, because to destroy or irreparably damage the larger group is a betrayal of not only that group but also oneself. It is clear how this applies for GCRs, particularly existential ones. If a possible outcome is the irretrievable collapse of civilisation or the extermination of the human species, one's own interests and those of everyone else are so entailed in the collective interest of the species that thinking about the question in cost–benefit terms simply does not make sense.

The second problem is a focus on the present or the short term – perhaps a matter of a few decades – at the expense of the longer term (Fisher 2019). It may be that those making the choices have no meaningful interest in the longer term. But a rational reason for adopting this approach might seem to be that because the future is unknowable beyond a very short time horizon, it makes sense to either not consider it at all or to apply a very large discount to anticipated future gains and losses. Alternatively, because most GCRs have either low probabilities or indeterminate probabilities so that there is no way of determining their likelihood, it may seem appropriate to ignore them.

Quite clearly, in reality, we *have* shown that we value what may happen only in the far distant future. Human beings of various eras and places have embarked on major building or other projects that would not be completed within the lifetimes of any one generation, often for hundreds of years. The most often cited example is that of medieval cathedrals, but this phenomenon is not confined to medieval Christianity. For example, the Temple of Apollo at Didyma was built over the course of several centuries and was still not complete at the time of its abandonment in the late Roman Empire.

In terms of GCRs, though, dealing with them or thinking about how to do so is not taken seriously by many economists, because it involves expending resources in the here and now to deal with something that may never happen or is most likely to happen well beyond the lifetimes of those now alive. The attitude is that the distant future should be left to look after itself, with many taking the attitude ascribed to Jeremy Bentham when asked why he took no account of posterity: 'What has posterity ever done for me?'

This obtuseness regarding costs and risks (or, for that matter, benefits) that are temporally distant or indeterminate comes from focusing purely on the interests of choosers in the here and now who are assumed to have no interests or concerns beyond the immediate. It ignores dynastic thinking and the way in which people are often concerned for the existence and flourishing of their descendants or of entities of which they are a part and which will continue to exist long after they are dead – the human species or civilisation as a whole being the case in point here. *Après moi le déluge* was seen as an irresponsible and selfish attitude when ascribed to Louis XV, but it is no less true now. This way of thinking derives in turn from perhaps the fundamental reason for contemporary economics having so little to say about questions such as GCR, which is a mistaken idea of methodological individualism. (It was once very much not the case for economists, as recently as the 1960s and 1970s, but time has moved on since then.)

For the great majority of economists, methodological individualism is one of the foundations of the discipline. This means looking at the actual choices about the allocation of resources and, indeed, anything with an economic aspect (i.e. most of life) as being carried out in the final analysis by *individuals*. Specific individuals make choices between different alternatives, and they do so to realise personal goals or to address specific personal needs, wants, feelings or desires. All of this is quite reasonable, and at the micro-level, when trying to explain why individuals or very small groups act in the ways that they do, it makes sense.

There are, of course, choices that are made by a collective decision-making process and these are the subject of the subdiscipline of public choice, which works by assuming that the best way to explain decisions made through such processes is by looking at the interests and choices of individual actors, such as politicians, bureaucrats and voters. This again makes sense because processes of this kind are carried out within an institutional framework (e.g. the electoral system and voting procedures) in which individuals make a choice with the institutions then aggregating those choices in a rule-bound way.

However, in economics and the social sciences there is a profound difference between processes and actions of the micro-level and collective rule-bound and those of larger or macro-level phenomena. The outcomes and workings of large-scale social processes involving many individual choices are ultimately opaque and mysterious. Crucially, and despite what many economists, political scientists and sociologists believe, they cannot be reduced to the aggregation of the multitude of personal choices. It makes sense to think of market outcomes, changes in the patterns and frequency of criminality, or movements of fashion and taste, for example, as being emergent phenomena, but the way that they emerge and the connection or mechanism between the emergent macro-level phenomena and the micro-level phenomena are usually impossible to discern.

One reason for this is that such processes are subject to butterfly effects (extreme dependence upon often trivial initial conditions) and complex and reflexive feedback loops. Another way of putting this is that wholes are more than just the sum of their individual parts but have qualities that cannot be reduced to the features and qualities of the individuals. This is the difference between a single ant or bee and an anthill or hive, between an individual wildebeest and a herd, or an individual human and a society or the species.

The problem is that for a generation or more, economists have tried to reconcile macro-level analysis with the micro-level by insisting that macro thinking has to have micro-level foundations. (An analogy in physics is the so-far unsuccessful attempt to reconcile quantum mechanics with relativity theory and cosmology.) This means that macro-level analysis is conducted in a way that makes it a summation or agglomeration of micro-level analysis and that large aggregates such as societies or electorates are treated and analysed as though they are comparable in their nature to individuals such as politicians.

This clearly causes problems when thinking about global or large-scale collective phenomena of any kind, not just GCRs – that is merely an extreme case. In the context of GCRs, it means treating the entire planetary population as though its interests are a summation or averaging of the interests and wishes of the individual people who compose it – by analogy, this is like treating an organism as a collection of cells rather than as a complex system or an entity in its own right. Clearly, that analogy has problems in the opposite direction as well because individual cells do not have agency or choice in any meaningful sense, while this is true of people as individuals, but that tells us that we are dealing with something complex, where neither strict holism nor definite individualism is appropriate. Specifically, this leads to the trait already mentioned, that of treating civilisation or the human species as being composed for practical purposes of those people now alive with the interests of future generations radically discounted.

The way this leads perceptive and thoughtful economists astray can be seen for example in recent essays by Daron Acemoglu. In one essay, he addresses the arguments of Toby Ord and others like him who are concerned about GCRs (Acemoglu 2021). The thrust of Acemoglu's argument is that we should not devote too much time or attention to GCRs (AI in particular), because if we do so, it will distract us and divert resources from other more pressing and soluble challenges, such as dealing with the economic impact of AI, and that if we are concerned with maximising human well-being in the here and now, that is what we should focus on.

This makes perfect sense from the perspective described but is obtuse, given what has already been set out about the reasons for taking events with ruinous downsides seriously. At one point, Acemoglu (2021) says, 'I would prefer that the public debate focus much more on the problems that AI is already creating for humanity, rather than on intriguing but improbable tail risks.' He then asks, 'Why should trying to eliminate future existential risks be given a superordinate priority over all other efforts to ameliorate the ills and suffering that our current choices are generating now and in the near term?'

This misses the point. In the first place, the argument as made here assumes that being concerned with tail risks such as unaligned AI is necessarily at the expense of, and as an alternative to, being concerned with immediate problems, such as the impact of AI on employment. This is simply not true. It is perfectly possible to be concerned with both and to devote resources intellectual and physical to both. This is like saying that you should not take out an insurance policy against the low risk of your house being completely destroyed because it will stop you redecorating. That would only be true if the cost of the first kind of concern and action was so high that it prevented the second, but this is rarely if ever the case.

Moreover, the kinds of action involved are often nested and complementary so that action to address an immediate problem can, so long as an eye is kept on the tail risk, actually contribute to protecting against the tail risk or making it less likely, while actions to mitigate or eliminate tail-end risks will often result in being better able to address the immediate challenges. Taking measures to mitigate the risks of misuse of AI in the immediate present, such as its being used for detailed control and surveillance, and improving its design to make it more aligned with general human interests, will both reduce immediate problems and make the catastrophic risk less likely. In addition, working out how to prevent the chances of unaligned or hostile AI will involve thinking better about how to devise and apply AI in ways that will make its impact more beneficial and more subject to conscious choice on our part. In other words, it is not an either-or choice.

More fundamentally, even if the risk is a tail risk, and so low probability, by definition if it happens, it will cost us everything, including all of the benefits gained from concentrating on the immediate and short-term problems in the meantime. This is like the investment that gives a decent and high-probability return in most years but has a low probability in any year of a catastrophic loss that wipes out all the previous profit and the capital (Taleb 2012). It is no good working on all of the immediate challenges posed by the implementation of AI if eventually the low-probability event of a malign and very powerful AI comes to pass because nothing has been done to think about or prevent it. In that case, all of those benefits are moot, because the human species has been wiped out.

The rejoinder is that the costs of taking effective action against the tail risk may be simply too high and cause damage that is so negative that it is better to accept the low probability of a disastrous outcome. Even granting that there is a mutually exclusive relationship between taking action about the tail risk and addressing the immediate problems, this is still a faulty argument. Acemoglu (2021) puts it this way:

> For the sake of argument suppose we could significantly reduce the probability of our own extinction by enslaving the majority of humankind for the next several centuries. Under Ord's lexicographic ordering, we would have to choose this option, because it minimises existential risk while still preserving humanity's potential to flourish fully at some point in the distant future.

This does not attack the actual argument Ord is making but rather: 'The argument for taking action to address existential risks could in extremis mean that we would be obliged to do something terrible. Therefore, we should not take that action.' That argument is only correct if the extreme action (enslaving humanity for several centuries) is the most likely or the necessary outcome of taking preventive action. To say that an argument can be used to justify an extreme action does not mean that it is therefore invalid as an argument in all cases. (Ord, of course, is not arguing that this kind of action should be taken or will be required, so this is also a straw man unless you can show that it will be needed despite what he says.)

Suppose the argument (which is closer to the actual one but still more extreme) was this: 'If, in order to prevent a GCR (whether it is an unaligned AI, or a climate flip), we have to take action that will reduce growth for several centuries, we should take that hit.' There is still an argument to be had there but the case is now not so obvious, to put it mildly. This is the real target of most economists' arguments, not the straw man target of doing something utterly appalling because it would head off a GCR – that would be justifiable only if there was no other way of doing it, only if there was a near certainty that it would work, and only if the risk was so imminent that there was no time to take any other type of action.

In other words, the presumptions set out earlier have come into play. The faulty understanding of risks, the focus on the short term and the misapplication of methodological individualism lead to the following actual view. 'It is wrong to be concerned with GCR if to do so means taking steps that will cause us to forgo benefits and incur costs in the here and now or the medium-term future – so we should take those benefits, not incur those costs, and let the tail risks look after themselves.'

All of this illustrates misapplication of the discount principle. This is a wider problem than the general economist's approach to GCRs. It is also true for less serious problems, such as systemic risk in areas such as financial markets. It is also a problem when considering the mirror image of GCRs, long-shot research, or investment that has little chance of immediate payoff but will yield spectacular results if it does (low-probability events with very large positive payoffs should they happen). Interestingly and revealingly, investment markets are more inclined to make investments in projects of that kind and to take account of low-probability or uncertain but massive downstream costs than are academic economists.

The problem is that there is an argument to be had about how to deal with GCR where economics can contribute in important ways (see, for example, Bourne 2021). One of the commonly suggested ways of responding to GCR is to ban or block certain kinds of scientific research or investigation. This has been suggested with AI, gene modification, research into pathogens, and nanotechnology, which would mean forgoing the potential future benefits from such research. In other cases, such as an abrupt shift in climate, it has been suggested that significant and costly changes be made to many features of the current economy. It may be that costs of this kind have to be borne to avoid existential and catastrophic tail risks, but you cannot make an informed decision about such matters unless you have an idea about the costs and know what it is you are doing, which means you need economics.

In addition, while it is mistaken to think that catastrophic tail risks should be simply disregarded in favour of concentrating on near-term and higher probability benefits, it is also an error to believe that *any* tail risk justifies imposing severe costs on the present. The path to take is, in some ways, to return to the outlook and intellectual frame of the classical economists. A central part of classical political economy (as its practitioners called it) was to think about the best way of ordering economic and political affairs so as to produce the best results in the long term – this was true for people as varied as Adam Smith, Malthus, Say, Mill and Marx. The key idea is that as well as analysing and advising on the present, the economist should be concerned with the management of entities that will exist beyond the life of anyone currently alive (most obviously, political communities).

Applied to this question, provided we think about the risks correctly, economics helps us to flesh out five areas.

1. It helps everyone better understand the costs involved with all courses of action. As such, it identifies the big challenge, which is to help find out responses to GCRs that do not impose very severe costs or are actually counterproductive – so avoiding the kind of stark choice posed in Acemoglu's argument. It helps enormously with the consequent challenge of doing this in such a way that more immediate problems are not ignored and identifies how to combine addressing the two. It can also help to identify the genuine hard cases, where heading off or mitigating a GCR will mean accepting a cost, even a high one, and will help with seeing how to minimise those costs.

2. Economic thinking can help us to identify the phenomena that may stop effective action on GCRs. Too many of those exercised by a perceived GCR (most notably, but not only, climate change) assume that the main obstacles to effective action are ill-will and selfishness. This produces a self-defeating and ineffectual politics and rhetoric. It also tends to be combined with a belief that the political process and state action are the best or only ways to deal with these and other problems, which itself presumes public motives will be public spirited. Sometimes this will be true, but the harsh reality is that power attracts rent-seekers, regardless of whether it is public or private.

There is a need, in other words, to move beyond that particular dichotomy and to think in terms of people responding to incentives as opposed to acting on motives. That suggests inter alia that the price mechanism is probably our most effective tool for dealing with many social problems, including several GCRs. Identifying through the economic point of view what the real problems preventing actions are helps in devising more effective ways of dealing with GCRs because they will get around these obstacles. These real problems include coordination and collective action, 'prisoner's dilemmas', the incentives facing politicians and, possibly, investors in the present institutional setting, and problems of externalities.

3. This means that economic thinking identifies the structural or systemic features of contemporary government, politics and economy that make GCRs more likely and successful preventive action less likely. For example, these include excessive top-down planning and

management and associated uniformity; an intellectual focus on certainty and forecasting or prediction as opposed to accepting uncertainty; designing systems for efficiency rather than adaptability and responsiveness; too much emphasis on maximisation of various metrics, which comes from excessive reliance on an explicit and quantifiable knowledge; not enough thinking about the longer term; and, at a societal level, the decay of institutions that lead to longer-term thinking.

4. It is economics that can lead to better understanding of the nature of innovation and the innovative process. This is hugely important because it is only innovation that will enable us as a species to avoid many of the GCRs without running crippling costs, or indeed at all. We should not assume that innovations will simply spring up like mushrooms when there is a need for them. The reality, as economic history demonstrates, is that sustained innovation is an exceptional event in most of human history before the modern era and that it requires a particular kind of cultural and institutional setting (Ridley 2020). There is also evidence that increasing complexity reduces returns to innovation as one of its effects (Strumsky et al. 2010). A more sophisticated argument, made by Mariana Mazzucato, is that innovation comes from directed, organised and purposive projects or actions by a partnership of governments and large firms. But this is also mistaken, and economics (and the evidence of history) suggests that what is needed is something quite different.

5. The specific question of the economics of innovation bears expansion. We have already argued that

consideration of the nature of extreme events with high costs leads to a moderated version of the precautionary principle. Thinking about those risks and bringing economic insights to bear, particularly those concerned with innovation, leads to another principle. This was first formulated by the expatriate British philosopher Max More as the 'proactionary principle' (Fuller and Lipinska 2014) . When he first set it out, it was aimed at the extreme or unqualified version of the precautionary principle, which was starting to gain notice at that time. In More's original formulation, the proactionary principle was an explicit contrast to the precautionary principle and directly opposed to it. However, the two are not inherently exclusive and, I would argue, the modified precautionary principle and the proactionary principle are actually complementary. Each requires the other for full effectiveness and realisation. What, though, is the proactionary principle? As formulated by More (2013), it includes the following elements.

> People's freedom to innovate technologically is highly valuable, even critical, to humanity. This implies several imperatives when restrictive measures are proposed: assess risks and opportunities according to available science, not popular perception. Account for both the costs of the restrictions themselves, and those of opportunities forgone. Favour measures that are proportionate to the probability and magnitude of impacts, and that have a high expectation value. Protect people's freedom to experiment, innovate, and progress.

What this means is that the possible benefits of innovation are so great that they should not be forgone unless there is clear evidence of a definite risk of sufficient severity associated with a particular innovation. Innovation is the key to resolving problems, including those that can be seen to arise from the innovative process. Any full accounting of human potential and flourishing must include the possible transformative impacts of certain innovations on the human condition. This in turn leads to action points: we should clearly identify risks in advance but usually do so in order to see where innovation is needed to head them off or mitigate their impact; we should think of risk and uncertainty as opportunities rather than just as challenges or problems; in the case of GCRs, we should look to see how we might take advantage of these risks as well as responding to them in preventive ways.

7 ACTIONS WE CAN AND SHOULD TAKE WITH REGARD TO GLOBAL CATASTROPHIC RISKS

The combination of the modified precautionary and proactionary principles leads to clear conclusions as to what actions we might take with regard to GCR. Some of these are general and may be thought of as principles that should guide policy in this area and, indeed, in many other areas as well. In fact, they are generic principles that people should be thinking of applying to a wide range of policy areas and not only the ones that can be considered as GCRs. Others are more specific and apply to particular cases of GCR. Before addressing this question, though, the terms 'us' and 'we' should be unpicked and defined. Throughout this work, I have argued that 'we' should act or be concerned about GCRs. Who or what though is the 'we' and who exactly is doing the acting?

Who is 'we'?

Ultimately, the 'we' in this account is the entire human species, considered as a single entity with a single or common interest. This is not the same thing analytically as the idea that all human beings as individuals have universal interests or goods because there are generic goods and bads for all humans (things that by their nature are good or bad for all people anywhere and everywhere). It is the idea that the shared and common interests of all of the human beings now existing, and their possible descendants, are so significant that we can reasonably speak of the interests of the human species as a whole, so that it is a single entity, analytically speaking.

Such an identity and interest has not always existed, because for most of human history the number and physical dispersion of human beings were such that they did not constitute a single entity with an identifiable single interest. The reason for this, in addition to there being a sufficiently large number of people widely dispersed, was that they were not sufficiently connected or affected by what the rest of the species did for there to be meaningful commonality of interest. The modern world, however, has seen this change. There is now in a very real sense a single global society and economy. The argument here is not that there is a global society in the sense of a subjective feeling of shared identity and interest, held by the majority of the global population; it is that the level and intensity of economic integration and division of labour is such that you have a single economic community or economic system. The problem is precisely that this objectively and physically existing integration and community is not matched by political integration or subjective identity, which is why you cannot expect political processes to address these kinds of problems (because of collective action problems, prisoner's dilemmas, etc.). This was precisely the issue in 1914, where Europe had become highly economically integrated (and with complete freedom of movement, much more so than today), but (obviously!) this was not matched in the political and social spheres. The result was disastrous.

This idea of a commonality of interest is clearly related to the category of GCRs because it is the global interconnectedness of human beings and the existence of a single society, along with the way this has happened, that makes many events *global* catastrophic risks that would not have been so in the past. Conversely, it is the threat posed by various GCRs to the well-being of all human beings, now and in the possible futures, which makes the idea of a single global human identity and interest more solid and the need to realise it more pressing.

This then, however, poses an obvious question and challenge. If there is a true global community and it makes sense to think of the totality of humanity as being a single entity in some respects (and so something for which the pronoun 'we' is appropriate), then what is the form that action, by the species as a whole, takes? When I and others say 'we need to do this or that', who exactly is the 'we' that is doing the acting?

At a more local level, the usual answer is the entity that is the active form or aspect of the collective entity or 'we' – a political one. In the modern world, that means a sovereign state. In a political entity, a select group of people take decisions on behalf of, and in the name and assumed interests of, a collective entity with a common identity and interest. This is usually a nation in the contemporary world but need not be, as the example of empires (by definition multinational and multicultural) shows. The people who act come to have that position through a variety of means, ranging from democratic politics, heredity or intrigue to simple force or conquest.

This means that one way of understanding 'we', meaning the entire human species, and how we should act is that action should be taken by sovereign states or, more precisely, the select people who control them. This has certain clear advantages. The institutions for doing this exist and, because of certain capacities at their disposal not legally available to other institutions or people (the ability to create money and the disposal of deadly force), they can implement measures that other kinds of entity cannot. Undoubtedly, much has to be done through this mechanism, for want of more effective alternatives.

However, there are at least three very serious drawbacks to this. The first being the weaknesses of the collective or political decision-making process identified by the scholars of public choice (Buchanan and Tullock 1999) – including rational ignorance, free-rider effects, and the capture of the decision-making process by specific interest groups because of the problem of concentrated benefits and dispersed costs or its inverse of concentrated costs and dispersed benefits (this is relevant for many of the measures that should be taken to address GCRs). What advocates of using the political process and acting through states should realise is that these problems are endemic to the process itself: they are not the result of ill-will or bad motives nor of the weaknesses of specific individuals or of certain ideologies and ideas – they will still exist regardless (Pennington 2010).

The second challenge in relying on sovereign states to deal with GCRs (or indeed other threats to the interests of all human beings) is the fundamental problem of knowledge. As Hayek argued, the nature of human knowledge, which is that the bulk of it is dispersed, local and tacit (meaning incapable of being captured in words or numbers), along with the inherently complex nature of social phenomena and processes, means that all institutional actors face intractable problems of ignorance, of simply not knowing enough to be able to plan or act effectively. Sometimes there is no alternative to acting in ignorance but, in that case, you have to expect that most acts will fail to achieve their desired outcome. This is true for *all* large and formally structured organisations and not just government. So this is an argument for not expecting too much from large organisations in general, including large firms or organisations. It is more acute for governments, however, because of the scale involved.

The third problem is even more fundamental. If the human species has in some ways a single identity and interest and if the political process is the way chosen to decide about and act on behalf of that interest and identity, then logically there should be a single agency to do this. That would mean a world state. This could be democratic in some way or it could be a world empire. The obvious problems are as follows: (a) it is hard to see how such an entity could come into existence in time to deal with the challenges, other than by a highly destructive process; (b) the threat it would pose to liberty and human flourishing would be immense, so much so that this would be a case of the cure being worse than the disease; (c) it would itself be an example of a GCR, that of a global and very long-lived tyranny; (d) the problems of public choice and knowledge already mentioned would be several orders of magnitude worse than they are for existing states, where they are bad enough already.

That leads to the belief, widespread since as far back as Henry IV of France, that the solution is to have an institutional arrangement, binding together sovereign states so that they act collectively in pursuit of shared interests and goals or even a single global goal (such as dealing with a GCR). This has been given expression in a series of institutions and treaties since 1944 and is at the heart of many current efforts to deal with GCRs. These are important and necessary, but we should not expect too much from them or rely upon them to the exclusion of other mechanisms.

The difficulty is that, while there is a common interest in addressing certain problems, the ruling groups in each sovereign state have their own specific interests. This, and the lack of any effective enforcement mechanism to punish those who break agreed rules, means that at a collective level sovereign states (or more accurately, their ruling groups) face a prisoner's dilemma, where acting rationally in their own interest will result in a general outcome that is bad for the general interest.

All this suggests that, while using the political process and acting through governments is inevitable and necessary, it should not be the primary way of acting, much less the only one. The 'we' that is the common interest of the species in survival and flourishing has to find other ways of acting, and other ways of defining the acting 'we'. The social sciences, including economics, suggest the way forward here.

Which is for private, voluntary and cooperative action to be the way of addressing this and other challenges. ('Private' includes everything from individuals or households to large corporations and other (non-commercial) non-governmental organisations.) Actions of this kind are aggregated and sometimes coordinated through social institutions. One obvious case is that of markets and prices, but social networks of various kinds exist, particularly the kinds of arrangements identified and studied by the late Elinor Ostrom and her students (Ostrom 2015).

One way that we can act, therefore, is through markets and the price mechanism. This runs against the common perception that the challenges posed in reacting to the threat of catastrophic risks lead inexorably to restricting private initiative. Quite apart from the arguments against relying on the political process set out above, there are positive reasons for thinking that markets and the price mechanism are an essential institution in this area. The price mechanism and market incentives have shown themselves to be by far the most effective way to bring about large-scale changes in behaviour, which may be needed to deal with some GCRs. They are also more effective in dealing with specific challenges, by leading people to abandon some harmful practices or adopt less harmful ones. Most importantly, it is the combination of experiment and investigation with market exchange and free institutions that is the source of sustained innovation. With the world faced with the threat of GCRs, innovation is needed more than ever, as is adaptability on the part of society and its systems – and markets win hands down on that.

Related to this is the need for entrepreneurial activity and discovery as part of the proactionary principle, to identify problems such as those posed by AI, and to arrive at solutions and protections. Entrepreneurialism in this context does not only mean private and profit-motivated action. Social action of all kinds can also be thought of this way, insofar as it involves thinking up innovative ways of dealing with identifiable challenges while at the same time seeking to be as effective as possible in terms of the relation between inputs and results. It has already been noted that many of those involved in thinking about GCR, such as Toby Ord, are also prominent figures in the Effective Altruism (EA) movement. This is not a coincidence as EA is a form of social entrepreneurialism, and social entrepreneurialism is one of the most effective responses to social problems, including risks such as GCRs (MacAskill 2015).

The institutional form for much of this is action by business corporations and capital markets – plus the entire area of decentralised, localised and networked social action and rule creation, meaning social action that is neither government-organised nor -funded nor profit-guided. This includes the kinds of institutions and rules for dealing with common access resources that were identified and studied by Elinor and Vincent Ostrom and are an important way of dealing with many social problems, including several GCRs (Ostrom 2012; Ostrom and Ostrom 2014). Anthropogenic climate change is one, but the most important is in checking or undoing the increasing systemic rigidity and fragility that are making many GCRs either more likely or more damaging.

There is also the whole area of personal and small group action, at the local, household or individual level. A GCR, by its nature, can seem to be far beyond the scope of such action. First, however, individuals and households can take measures on their own account to protect themselves against GCRs. The point is that actions taken at the personal level add up if the numbers are large enough. Second, it is individual and local action that is the foundation for the larger-scale social action referred to above – those things will not happen without it – so it should not be discounted.

All this suggests, finally, what the role of the political process should be, in this as in other matters. There will be some areas where, because of severe collective action problems, political action such as laws and regulations are needed, but the aim should be to minimise these. Where politics is essential is in creating the institutions and rules that make social action possible.

General principles and guidelines

With all that has been said in mind, what then are the principles that should shape the form that responses of all kinds to GCR should take?

Make bets rather than forecasts

One principle has already been mentioned more than once. In thinking about risk of any kind but GCR in particular, there is no point in making forecasts or prognostications. Trying to predict what will happen is a waste of time, and attempting to put a date on such forecasts is even worse. The quest for certainty is futile. A better way of approaching the making of decisions about GCR is to think of it as a bet; the decision should be whether to take the bet and the possible consequences of it not working out (Duke 2018). As with regular insurance, we need to multiply the loss of welfare associated with an event by the probability of its happening. This in turn tells you what kind or level of costs it makes sense to incur as a protection or hedge against the risk. Where the cost would be ruinous for humanity or civilisation as a whole, then even low probability may mean that action needs to be taken. This clearly poses two further questions.

- How do you establish the odds?
- How do you ensure that those making the decisions about what to do once the odds are established also have a stake in the outcome?

So, first, how do you establish the odds? Fortunately, there are two simple and well-established methods. The first is to use a prediction market such as Metaculus. Here people make predictions as to the likelihood of something happening, or of the time frame within which they expect it to happen, or for whether some statement will prove to be true or not. This builds on the DELPHI model of strategic forecasting developed by the RAND Institute during the Cold War. Frequently, those making the prediction put up a stake, with the pool of money generated by the stakes going to those with the most accurate expectations/predictions if the event comes to pass or if there is a decisive call as to the truth or otherwise of the statement. The predictions are aggregated and averaged out to give an overall prediction, expressed as a percentage.

The second, more useful method is a large, liquid betting market. This may seem strange to many (unless they are themselves aficionados of gambling). Bets are wagers where money is staked between participants on the course of future events or on whether or not something will happen. Bets can be taken also on the scale of an event (e.g. the margin of victory in an election, or a football game) through the mechanism of spread betting. The odds offered for a bet are flexible and are generated by the amount of money wagered on a particular outcome – the more that is placed on a particular outcome or event, the shorter the odds. Odds are therefore the prices that reflect the expectations of the participants (the betters) as to the probability of an event. They thus have a broad predictive capacity, in the same way that prices in a futures market do. Their flexibility enables them to respond, often rapidly and sharply, to changes in circumstance and to new information. Most importantly, the record of betting at predicting futures is vastly superior to other forms of forecasting, and is much better than expert prognostications. This makes formalised betting markets the best tool there is, on the evidence, for establishing the probability of future events. Prediction aggregators are also useful as a different way of gauging or establishing expectations.

Bets on possible disasters have already been made on a small scale, often between individuals. To take a well-known case, Sir Martin Rees and Steven Pinker entered into a public wager with the following terms.[1] The bet was that 'a bioterror or bioerror will lead to one million casualties in a single event within a six-month period starting no later than Dec 31, 2020'. The stake was $400, with Rees betting for and Pinker against. The term has expired, but the two parties have agreed to extend the term until there is sufficient clarification as to whether the Covid pandemic originated in a lab leak – if that proves to be the case, then Rees will collect. The bet was placed on LongBets, a site that specialises in wagers of this kind.

What is needed to make this more useful is firstly a much larger number of participants – personal bets like the one between Rees and Pinker do not tell us anything significant about probability. Also, the market needs to be one where actual money is traded (as opposed to being a prediction summary process like Metaculus), and like all markets, it needs to be liquid so as to enable shifts in prices (odds) in response to new information or events. The need for liquidity means that a large amount of money needs to be involved. Perhaps more controversially, there should also be a limit on the speed of transactions to stop ultra-rapid trades where the object of the trades and speculation is not the underlying bet but the market itself. Trading of this kind can lead to positive feedback loops

1 Martin Rees and Steven Pinker: wagering on catastrophe. *New Statesman*, 16 June 2021 (https://www.newstatesman.com/politics/uk/2021/06/martin-rees-and-steven-pinker-wagering-catastrophe).

that lead to spikes and crashes where there is no new information or events and also increases the amount of noise in the signal the betting market produces. There should also be a secondary market, a way of both trading and 'laying' the bets. In regular betting this is done through secondary markets such as Betfair.

This idea of using a betting market and gambling as a way to inform policy (and not only in this area) may seem a fringe novelty, but it should not, as this is actually a well-established principle: insurance and reinsurance markets, for example, are essentially elaborate markets in wagers. One of the most important features is the 'wisdom of crowds' effect, in which the aggregate odds produced by bets made by a large number of people, many (or most) of whom are ignorant about the subject matter of the bet, are more accurate than predictions by experts. In fact, the higher the proportion of experts, the worse the accuracy (Surowiecki 2005). Another aspect of gambling-based prediction markets is that if people are gambling with their own money, then they have skin in the game because they not only stand to gain if they get it right, but they also face loss if they get it wrong. This adds to their accuracy.

Second, how do you ensure that those making the decisions about what to do once the odds are established also have a stake in the outcome? These people are, of course, not necessarily involved in the predictive market. The key thing here is to ensure that those making the decisions (apart from the gamblers in the prediction market) face costs as well as benefits – they will pay a price if they get it wrong or reap gains should they get it right (Taleb 2018).

This is very important because there is overwhelming evidence that in cases where this does not apply, the quality of decision-making declines massively. A key measure is therefore to insist as far as possible that those making decisions have significant exposure to a prediction market as to the results of their decisions.

Rely mainly upon tinkering, rather than mega-projects, and decentralised and varied networks, rather than top-down and uniform structures and processes

Faced with a threat that is by definition global, the temptation is to look for a global solution. This is often combined with a second temptation, to aim for large-scale and institutional methods of addressing the problem or challenge.

On the one hand, we should usually follow a quite different strategy when dealing with GCRs, one that makes use of localised and decentralised networks and relies upon the experimentation and tinkering of large numbers of individuals and small organisations rather than large 'projects'. The problems of knowledge and coordination faced by all large organisations are even worse at a global level, quite apart from the political difficulty of reaching agreement in some cases.

On the other hand, many of the concrete actions and responses needed to head off GCRs need to be taken throughout the world if they are to be effective, so it would seem that we face an intractable dilemma. The dilemma is only apparent, however. It arises from thinking that the only choice lies between global or supranational political and governance action on the one hand, and action by particular sovereign states on the other. A recent work on climate change takes this starting point and argues that the only effective way to address this is by nationalism and strengthening the nation state, and if you grant the premise that these are the only two choices available, it is convincing (Lieven 2020). There is, though, a third option, which is to make use of networks that arise from the bottom up and are coordinated by relations between the local nodes (localised groups or clearing houses) and that can now be coordinated on a global scale. This approach is much better at dealing with otherwise intractable knowledge problems.

It is also much better for the key issue of innovation of all kinds. Much of the current approach to major challenges such as anthropogenic climate change is dazzled by the example of the Manhattan and Apollo projects, which finds expression in Mariana Mazzucato's call for 'project government' (2021). In reality, what historical research shows is that innovation mainly comes from decentralised experimentation, in parallel, by large numbers of tinkerers who imitate and copy each other (Ridley 2020). This can be seen in a range of well-known historical examples such as electricity and telephony in the nineteenth century. With telephony, Alexander Graham Bell and his competitor Elisha Gray were only two of many figures who worked on the challenge. Many were exploring and developing the specific technologies that were needed for the telephone to be possible, such as converting sound into electrical signals in microphones and then converting the electricity back into sound. Importantly, many parallel avenues of enquiry were followed simultaneously and all of this tinkering led to progressive small-scale improvement and discovery, which is how most technological (and social) innovation happens, rather than in a single 'big bang'.

The Apollo and NASA example actually supports this, as the creation of NASA and the subsequent focus on one specific goal of getting a man to the Moon and back led to a focus on a specific suite of technologies, cutting short the previous more wide-ranging experimentation – this has now resumed with the advent of private-sector space exploration and technological development. The creation of NASA cut short the rival research projects of the US Army and Airforce. When this was combined with the single goal of getting a man to the Moon, the consequence was a focus on throwaway step rockets as the single most straightforward way of realising that goal. Other avenues, such as the X plane programme and the technologies it would have led to, such as reusable launchers and a permanent presence in near-Earth orbit, were abandoned. NASA crowded out private sector investigation of other kinds of motive power or methods of getting into orbit. It developed a nuclear engine for long-distance interplanetary travel but then abandoned it. Surprisingly, the creation of NASA and the Apollo project held back the development of space travel and associated technologies rather than assisting it, mainly by putting all technological and investigative eggs into one basket, which, to mix metaphors, turned out to be a blind alley for many purposes.

Have systemic features of resilience and adaptability (anti-fragility) rather than complexity and narrowly defined efficiency

One of the clearest conclusions that we can draw from the Covid pandemic is that many existing systems, from hospitals and social care to logistics and financial services, are excessively 'efficient'. In pursuit of a narrow definition of efficiency and return on assets, there has been a systematic stripping out of redundancy and extra capacity. Everything is taut with no slack – which means close to snapping point. This looks very good to accountants, but it also makes the systems involved very fragile and susceptible to breakdown when confronted with an unexpected shock.

Above all, it makes the prospect of a cascading systems failure much more likely and makes recovery from such a failure more difficult than it should be. It is time to relearn something the military has always known, that you have to expect the unexpected and that redundancy and having more than one plan is the way to go. This way of thinking can also apply to technology – it may seem natural and efficient to only have one technology and to abandon older ones completely as new ones arise. This strategy, however, is to run an enormous risk, of essentially putting all of one's eggs into one (often fragile) basket. It makes more sense to have several ways of acting side by side (e.g. to have more than one kind of transportation system), and it often makes sense to preserve and even continue to develop technologies that appear to be obsolete. Older technologies are often more robust and less liable to catastrophic systems failure than newer ones. The persistent trend, over the last 60 years in particular, towards greater complexity in both systems and technology, has frequently had the effect of making systems and devices harder to repair swiftly and more susceptible to being affected by systems failure.

There are several examples of technologies or systems that should be preserved. One, already mentioned, is cash as a payment medium. Another is landline telephony. In the area of maritime transport, it is worth keeping the technology of windjammers alive (these are very large sailing ships with steel hulls and masts and steel wire rigging). Steam power and hydraulic power are other examples, as is the rigid airship.

Have institutions and ways of living that lead to a focus upon the longer term and the trans-generational, rather than the immediate and short term, and upon the collective rather than the purely individual

As pointed out earlier, a major problem with thinking about GCRs, particularly but not solely among economists, is a focus on the immediate and short term and a refusal to even consider longer-term and trans-generational costs and benefits. This is a serious problem in other areas of public policy as well, such as pensions, social care and government liabilities. The lazy assumption is that this derives from an inherent human predilection for the short term, but the evidence of history is that this is not so; there are many examples of investment and other projects where the return is multi-generational. In purely mathematical terms, a low or modest return over a long period or a very low return over an indefinite period are the same as a high return over a short period.

The current intellectual and practical focus on high short-run returns comes from a number of historically specific factors, notably a deranged monetary policy since at least the early 1990s, and the undermining by public policy of the family as an institution – the problem here is the focus on the personal and the immediate rather than dynastic or familial thinking that looks at generations. Linked to this is an excessive individualism, which sees happiness and flourishing in purely individual terms and ignores the reality that these depend upon the well-being of larger social aggregations in which individuals are embedded and that partly define the nature and prospects of individuals. Addressing these questions is beyond the scope of this essay, but it is clear that if humanity is to successfully get past the possible 'Great Filter' of GCRs, then there has to be a return to the more historically normal pattern of long-term and multi-generational thinking. Part of this involves creating or restoring institutions so that they exist for more than a single generation and reversing the policy and institutional arrangements that have emphasised ephemerality rather than longevity (in firms, for example).

Allow for projects and responses to risks that have low probability of success but massive payoff if they succeed

We have been concerned with low-probability but catastrophic events, but it is important to remember their mirror image – that of low-probability events and outcomes that would have a very large and transformative positive effect if they were to happen. The important cases are not windfalls or flukes but long-shot investments or speculative investigations. Investment in projects that might deliver such results is a function of the size of the potential payoff multiplied by the estimated chance of it happening. If the payoff is sufficiently large (and a positive payoff could include preventing or precluding higher probability threats, such as certain GCRs), then it makes sense to invest large sums. This is what lies behind an idea that baffles many outsiders: the willingness of investors to put large amounts of money behind very speculative new technologies and innovations. Back in the 1950s, Robert Heinlein posited an institution dedicated to such investments and investigation with the Long Range Foundation (which had the motto 'Bread Cast Upon the Waters'), but, in fact, we now have a whole industry and specialised markets devoted to this (Heinlein 2016). It is this kind of institution and market that should fund areas such as investigation of fusion power and extra-planetary colonisation or a way of storing, transporting and compressing energy. Any one of these three, and particularly the last, would have a major impact on GCRs of various kinds. Projects of this kind are important for the future of humanity in general but particularly for heading off GCRs. The decentralised market model is better placed to succeed than a government project for the reasons I have already stated. Where governments can help in this is by offering significant inducements and incentives such as very large rewards or prizes (which are much more effective than intellectual property, which is almost certainly now a net drag on such investigation and investment).

Levels of response to global catastrophic risk

As well as looking at responses in terms of general principles, it also helps to categorise them in terms of how much, and what, can be done in response to different kinds of risk. The obvious limiting case is that of truly unknown risks. We can do only the absolute minimum about them. What of the known ones? We need to think about the levels or types of action that can be taken and to consider how effective they might be in relation to each kind of risk.

The first category of actions is those that if taken would eliminate the chance of the event happening at all or make it so trivial that it would cease to be a problem. The difficulty in many cases is that the action that would eliminate the risk entirely would also bring considerable costs. For example, a complete ban on all AI research would, if effective, obviously eliminate the risk from that kind of technology, but the costs in terms of forgone benefits would be enormous. In addition, it would make it more difficult to deal with some of the other GCRs discussed. Quite apart from all of that, there is the question of enforceability. The same argument applies to measures such as prohibiting all kinds of research involving gene editing. The calculation that has to be made is whether it would be worth incurring the costs to eliminate the risk. Sometimes it would be, and obviously in that case it would make sense to accept the costs of the actions. But sometimes the costs would be too great – above all where it means giving up the chance to have capacities that would make dealing with other GCRs easier. At that point, the yardstick becomes the relative estimated probability of different kinds of GCR. For example, AI will make dealing with climate change easier, so the question becomes which is more probable, a sudden climate reset, or AI leading to human extinction or the end of civilisation.

The second level is actions that would reduce the probability of a GCR happening to a much lower level. A reduction in probability also means that the time horizon over which we can say that the event is likely would become greater. This may mean a longer time in which to take action to eliminate the risk or to find other methods of resolving it. Again, there would be costs associated with actions of this type, but they would typically be less than in the first case. For example, bans on certain *types* of research as opposed to an entire *category* could reduce the chance of an accidental pandemic without eliminating that risk.

The third type or level of actions are those that would have no significant effect on the probability of an event happening but would mitigate its impact. This can be in terms of severity and/or scope. Regarding severity, the aim would be to reduce the impact from terminal or existential to endurable or even minor. In terms of scope, the aim would be to reduce the impact from global to regional or local. As previously noted, a classic example of this is the adoption of measures everywhere to manage the risk of epidemics following the Black Death. Measures such as quarantine meant that while epidemics of plague still occurred regularly, they did not develop into a global pandemic of the kind seen in the fourteenth century, and these measures also mitigated the impact at a local level. Measures that aim at reducing complexity and increasing the level of redundancy and failsafe features in complex systems also fall into this category. Something to note is that, when defined in this way, mitigation includes adaptation, changing arrangements so as to adapt to something and make its effects less damaging – climate change is the most obvious example but there are others.

The fourth type includes those where neither the chance of a GCR coming to pass would be reduced or eliminated, nor would the immediate effects be mitigated or reduced. Rather, the object would be to ensure the continuation of human life. The kind of actions we are speaking of here are often labelled 'monastery', 'Ark' or 'lifeboat' measures (Adapt Research 2019). The aim would be to ensure that at least enough people and other key species survive an extinction-level event for the human species to continue, or to ensure that, even if civilisation does collapse, critical knowledge and skills are preserved and transmitted so that it would reappear much sooner, or be capable of reappearing when otherwise it would not. Measures like this are a kind of mitigation, but in this case the only dimension of the GCR that would be mitigated is the duration of the effects rather than scope or severity.

Some points can be made here regarding this initial categorisation of possible responses. First, there is a rough relationship between the extent of the impact of these measures and their cost, both absolute and in terms of opportunity costs. 'Lifeboat' measures can be cheap and certainly less costly than the third type mentioned, which in turn are less expensive than the second, with the first type the most costly. Second, there are many different kinds of concrete actions or programmes that fit into the different types: these include research programmes, regulatory or legal changes, actual spending of resources on physical actions of various kinds, and institutional reforms. The main point, though, is that we can solve the various kinds of GCR by relevant types of response.

For some kinds of GCR, it is possible to take only the fourth kind of action. This is the case for some of the natural risks such as a supervolcanic eruption or natural climate change. However, the fourth kind of action can be taken for *all* of the risks identified here, apart perhaps from some of the highly speculative ones. There are then others where, in addition to the fourth, it is also possible or sensible to take the third type but not more than that. By progression, there are some where types two to four can be taken, and finally there are ones where all four can be. The point is that in these latter cases the different types or levels of precautionary action could all be taken simultaneously, as they are not mutually exclusive.

In fact, it makes more sense to think of them as nested, so that taking one type of measure involves also taking the less extensive ones. The major qualification to that is that the final category of 'lifeboat' measures is not nested within the other three but is rather something that should be used for any GCR – it is a kind of generic insurance against *any* kind of GCR. Even if the various levels of measure are not nested, it makes perfect sense if we are taking level one–type measures to also take levels two and three. The reason is that these lesser measures should be thought of as fallback measures should the highest level fail. Scepticism and probabilistic reasoning should lead us to think of measures to counteract GCRs as also being bets, on the chances of the measures working. Having a more moderate measure in place provides cover should the bet on the more radical measure working not come off.

More specific actions and responses

Natural, speculative and unknown risks

Regarding GCRs in these categories, with one significant exception, there is not much in the way of measures that human beings can take, given our current level of technology. Taking action that would eliminate the possibility of such an event or reduce its likelihood is not possible for events such as supervolcanic eruptions or gamma ray bursts. The main measures would be 'lifeboat', which would ensure key resources and knowledge were not irretrievably lost. They would establish highly secure stores throughout the world; each would contain recorded knowledge and useful information, so as to make technological recovery swifter, and resources of various kinds, such as seeds and genetic material. Such installations already exist – the Svalbard Global Seed Vault (which stores a vast array of seeds and plant materials) and the nearby Arctic World Archive (which is a major depository for information of a range of types, along with methods of accessing it).

We should build several such centres, located in areas that are geologically stable and in range of climate zones, so ensuring that at least one will survive a major catastrophic event, such as an asteroid impact or a natural climate flip. This action can be taken at relatively low cost and is important as the final line of defence against *all* kinds of GCR. As these facilities would need to be staffed and maintained, the supplementary part of such a programme would be to create small communities of volunteers who would live in and maintain the centres.

The other ultimate fallback is a technology that many want to pursue for quite different reasons – extraterrestrial colonisation. If self-sustaining colonies could be established elsewhere in the Solar System, this would provide one obvious hedge against GCRs, which is that the inhabitants would be able to escape the impact of events that affected only Earth. At present, humanity only has one place in the universe where it can survive, and this makes our species highly vulnerable. A programme of extra-planetary colonisation would take a considerable time to come to fruition, but it is still worth pursuing. It should be thought of as an example of the long-term and long-shot investments or projects that it makes sense to pursue.

There are two specific risks in this set of categories where more could theoretically be done in addition to the 'lifeboat' projects. The first is natural global warming, where it might be possible to mitigate the effects of a sharp natural reset of the planet's climate. This would essentially involve ensuring that systems are sufficiently adaptable, resilient, innovative and dynamic to respond to something like the relatively rapid onset of a new ice age or a sudden shift in the world's climate patterns to a warmer and more 'equable' equilibrium. There is little in the way of specific measures that could be taken, however, unlike in the case of an abrupt reset due to human activity, where we already have a clear idea of what is likely to happen and can design specific mitigating measures.

The other is that of an asteroid impact. Here the strange position is that there is little we can do in the way of mitigation but a lot we can do in terms of reducing the probability. If an asteroid above a certain size strikes the planet, the impact would be so devastating that mitigation would not be possible – we would only have the lifeboat measures to fall back on. However, there are several measures that could be taken to reduce the probability of that happening. One, already underway, is to systematically track and identify objects in the Solar System and to try as far as possible to predict which, if any, may become a cause for anxiety. This is a moving target because of new objects entering the Solar System or being discovered, and because of complex gravitational effects on the orbits of objects, which makes it a challenge to predict their movements. The second is to develop technology that will enable us to deal with all but the very largest asteroids and comets. This would require a permanent space-travelling facility as well as technologies, using, for example, nuclear explosions to shatter or divert threatening objects. As such, a programme of this kind would fit in and be part of the wider space exploration and development programme already mentioned.

Pandemics: natural and human-created or -facilitated

As already discussed, the threat of a devastating pandemic is highly topical. The chances of a natural pandemic on the scale of the Black Death are low (it is at most a 300-year event, so a 1 in 300 chance in any year), but it is still worth taking seriously. A pandemic caused by human folly or malevolence is a more serious risk both because the probability is more difficult to calculate and because such a pandemic has a higher chance of being truly devastating in terms of mortality than a natural one (Taleb et al. 2020b; Marani et al. 2021). Here elimination, reduction and mitigation all come into play. As explained, the three levels or types of response should not be seen as alternatives but as nested or parallel measures that complement each other.

At the level of elimination, the risk of a natural pandemic cannot be removed. The chance of an enhanced pandemic, one that is caused or exacerbated by human activity, can be removed, however, at least in theory. For this to happen, certain kinds of experimentation and investigation, such as gain-of-function experiments, would have to be completely prohibited on risk grounds, with the ban being made to stick. The case for doing this is overwhelming, on probabilistic precautionary grounds (Lipsitch 2018). The potential downside is so large that even when it is multiplied by a low probability, the outcome is huge. The potential benefits of this kind of research (better understanding of viral infections and how to combat them) are simply not large enough to outweigh this, not least because there are other, less risky, ways of achieving the same results. The problem is one of enforcement, as this would have to be universal for it to be effective. The evidence of the Biological Weapons Convention suggests that it may be possible to enforce such a rule, but the challenge is that it only needs one or two rogue actors to nullify it. This does not mean that the attempt should not be made, only that we should plan for it not working.

It is because some actions may not work that risk reduction and effect mitigation measures should also be taken. There are several measures that would significantly reduce the risk of a natural pandemic arising from zoonotic transmission. These would require major changes to certain parts of the economy. However, these are also measures that it makes sense to take for other reasons, quite independent of their impact on the probability of this particular GCR. The first is to reduce human pressure on wildlife habitats by the creation and enforcement of major nature reserves and by large enough payments or transfers to local populations to change their incentives so that they do not continue to encroach on the habitats. This is similar to other measures that can and should be undertaken to preserve threatened species, all of which involve using market mechanisms and incentives (as well as transfers via governments). The second is to take steps by a combination of regulation and technological innovation to do away with contemporary intensive livestock farming, because of its role as a location for the development and transmission of novel pathogens. A related measure (also relevant for other GCRs such as abrupt climate reset) would be to encourage the development of synthetic meat. In this case, there may be little need to introduce measures, as the technology and industry is rapidly developing anyway.

The mitigation measures are ones that in many cases are already in place – in theory. However, experience of the Covid-19 pandemic shows that much of this has existed on paper but has proved seriously lacking in practice. The major mitigation measures are those that will contain or slow down the spread of a novel pathogen. If sufficiently successful, they will stop an outbreak becoming truly global and so they can be positioned in the probability reduction class. They will also, however, make a pandemic that does happen easier to manage and less damaging. The foundational measure is an early warning system to detect the appearance of a novel pathogen at an early stage and track its spread. In theory, this is already in place, but it did not work correctly in the early stages of the Covid-19 pandemic, so clearly there needs to be major improvement. The second is the capacity to shut down most long-distance travel at short notice in large parts of the world should such a warning be given. This may sound costly and draconian but would actually reduce the need for more extensive (and more costly) measures of the kind we saw in 2019–21. There should also be provision for introducing health checks at short notice as a condition of international travel. This is related to the other important mitigatory step, which is to have a set of public health measures that would not normally be utilised in everyday life but that could be rolled out very swiftly. The most important of these is a way of identifying early cases and then swiftly tracing and isolating all of their contacts as quickly as possible, because if this can be done, then the spread can be contained or its rate reduced to a level that becomes more manageable without the need to resort to draconian measures such as lockdowns (only marginally effective anyway, on the evidence, and needed mainly because of systemic fragility, above all in healthcare).

The final mitigatory measure is the one bright point of the Covid pandemic, which is a system for the rapid development and deployment of effective prophylactic treatments such as vaccines. This is a classic illustration of one of the general strategic principles set out earlier, of relying upon decentralised networks and parallel experimentation for innovative responses rather than on large projects. It is this that makes possible trying out a number of avenues simultaneously, and, with Covid, was stunningly successful.

An anthropogenic climate reset

Climate change, even severe, that takes place over a sufficiently long timescale is not a catastrophic risk. That does not mean it is not something to worry about or that it is a minor problem, quite the contrary. It means only that it falls into the category of 'very severe but endurable' as opposed to catastrophic (terminal or existential). The real GCR is that of a relatively abrupt reset of the planet's climate to a hotter or more 'equable' equilibrium, due to tipping point effects. Further debate about this is otiose. This is not primarily a matter of the scientific consensus being overwhelming; it is rather a matter of the odds and the downsides of the implied bet not working out. The costs of a large rise in global temperature and, even more, of a rapid reset in the global climate are so large that even if the odds against its happening are very long, the expected loss is still so massive that it makes sense to take action.

The indications are that it is too late to completely avert significant anthropogenic climate change and that it is already well under way. The odds of stopping a significant reset in a short period of time (over one to two decades) in the near future are also getting longer (in other words, the likelihood that it will happen is rising). This means that measures to eliminate the chance of such a shift are getting steadily less likely to succeed. That does not mean, how-ever, that they should not be taken, because they will also assist with limiting and mitigating the scale and impact of a climactic reset and thus removing it from the category of catastrophic or existential to severe or very severe, but endurable. In thinking about abrupt climate reset, which is by far the most pressing GCR and the one with easily the highest probability of happening, the broad strategic prin-ciples set out earlier all come in to play – a situation where decentralised and network-based market and emergent solutions are needed more than ever. The requirement to think in multi-generational terms is also pressing as many of the mitigatory/adaptive actions in particular will only be effective over very long time horizons.

Many of the steps needed to reduce the probability of a reset and, should that fail, to mitigate its impact or adapt to the consequences, are obvious and have been extensively discussed. To look at the full range of decentralised and market solutions to this challenge would require a whole book or series of monographs. The point to make here is that as well as specific programmes and moves, whether produced by decentralised and market-driven action or government-led projects, there need to be actions that reset incentives and shift the overall framework within which actors do things.

The most obvious is to raise the cost of activities that contribute to the process. The evidence suggests that an escalating carbon tax is the best way of doing this, despite or even because of its being a blunt instrument. Raising costs of carbon use in this way is the simplest and most powerful way of making incentives and market mechanisms bring about rapid and large-scale shifts in behaviour (Johnson 2010). There are certain kinds of activity where a more rapid reset is needed and so additional measures are required, not so much because these activities are major contributors to the problem but because they are ones that are increasing in size at a rapid rate. One is travel, particularly air travel; the other is the growth of the Internet and online activity, which have very large and escalating energy costs. The main point is to take action through the taxation system, which raises the cost of high-energy usage, in addition to the impact of a carbon tax. The main point of a carbon tax, though, is not simply to raise costs; it is to enable people collectively to discover, through the price mechanism, just how much they are prepared to alter their present way of living to reduce emissions to a given level.

Right now, talk on this topic is cheap, because unpriced. A carbon tax will crystallise what the costs are in terms of forgone opportunities elsewhere of reaching a certain emissions level. This will concentrate minds and make decisions and discussions more informed and focused.

The best known step is to bring about a major reset in the energy supply system: this is under way, and the main focus is on a move to so-called renewable energy. This is much more problematic and challenging than many realise and will also require significant investment in and use of nuclear electricity generation – as a number of prominent environmental activists have realised.[2] The main challenge, however, is where, with current technology, renewable energy cannot replace fossil fuels, because it is too diffuse – industrial heating and much transport are the main examples of important activities (Smil 2021).

This difficulty is made more acute by the realisation that production of large quantities of products, including steel and cement, will be required for any transition, and this cannot be done economically without fossil fuels, as things stand. In addition, the production of cement inevitably leads to much carbon emission, even if it is undertaken with renewable energy (not possible at the moment). All of this suggests that the costs of an energy transition are far greater than any benefit as well as being ineffectual, given current levels of technology.

2   Nuclear power is the only green solution. James Lovelock website. Published in *The Independent*, 24 May 2004 (http://www.jameslovelock.org/nuclear-power-is-the-only-green-solution/).

This means that the major focus of the innovation and discovery process has to be on methods of storing and, above all, compressing energy, and it is here that the de-centralised ecosystem of innovation really comes into play. The main measures governments can take are to encourage this by incentives such as prizes and by rolling back excessive intellectual property protection.

Two of the longer-term management and mitigation measures would best be delivered by private and decen-tralised means but would need assistance from incentive-shifting governmental measures. First, increasing the density of urban settlement, and second, large-scale re-forestation – this is important here because of its wider cli-mate stabilisation effects and not primarily as as a means of carbon capture (Bendell 2023). Another step would be to encourage and accelerate the movement away from con-ventional intensive agriculture, particularly in livestock farming but also with regard to much arable farming (Monbiot 2023). An important part of this is reversing the regulatory and subsidy regime that has encouraged de-structive intensive farming (Body 1982). One route would be to increase energy inputs to food production by mov-ing away from conventional farming, but an alternative would be to shift a large part of the population back into labour-intensive agriculture, so recreating a peasantry (Heinberg 2006). There are some who favour this, but the social implications are transformative, to say the least.

There are also, of course, short-term mitigation meas-ures such as better flood defences and irrigation and water conservation measures, as well as making adaptations to changed conditions – making migration and resettlement easier, for example. Here there needs to be a combination of spontaneous or emergent processes and guidance or direction of those processes by government. 'Lifeboat' measures would be the ultimate fallback with an additional element concerning climate reset and some other GCRs. This is to deliberately preserve, possibly through the use of subsidies but also through action by voluntary groups, technologies that would survive a major simplification of civilisation and remain viable. One example is that of the use of wind power for long-distance maritime transport, in the shape of windjammers, but there are many others such as hydraulic power. It may seem strange to the accountant's mind, but it actually makes sense for a combination of governments and private action to keep such technologies alive by paying for the construction and use of windjammers or hydraulic power systems, for example, so that they run parallel to the currently dominant technologies but can be expanded if needed. This is not so different from the policy of continuing to invest in a railway system alongside the road network and not going down the route followed by the US of allowing the older system to atrophy almost completely.

Critical resource depletion

The challenge of critical resource depletion is less pressing and more easily resolved, as we have examples of how a decentralised market and social system can resolve this given the correct institutions. The latter though is key, as current trends in several areas show that the current institutional framework is not working. A market system and process of decentralised innovation will resolve challenges of resource depletion through greater efficiency, changes in use (including major reduction in many cases) and innovations that create substitutes for the resource in many uses – but only if the institutions and the incentives they create are working properly.

Water is a case in point. Depletion of water reserves is an increasingly serious problem in many parts of the world due to systematic overuse of fresh water, which occurs because water is not correctly priced, despite being an increasingly scarce resource relative to demand. As a result, it is overconsumed. If this were corrected, users would reduce consumption. Similarly, overexploitation of land leading to topsoil degradation and loss reflects the derangement of the price signal by public policies such as subsidies and regulation that aim to maximise production or to reward politically connected interests (Body 1982). It also reflects the way the current monetary and financial system incentivises short-term returns over longer-term ones. With fossil fuels there is both overuse, again due partly to subsidies and favourable tax treatment, and also a failure to respond to rising production costs because of the way current monetary policy has encouraged the exploitation of high-cost marginal sources and so headed off a sharp price rise. All of these are challenges that a market innovative system can resolve. The bad news is that unless the problems of mispricing are corrected by institutional reform, the processes will reach a tipping point where there will be a sudden catastrophic crisis. The good news is that, compared with other cases on this list, the action required is relatively simple, even if the consequences will be painful for many people in the short term.

Technological spillovers:
AI, genetic modification and nanotechnology

The area of technological spillovers such as 'unaligned' AI or the disastrous results of genetic modification or of a nanotechnology gone wrong may seem remote and fanciful. And yet these are the GCRs that most concern the experts and think tanks. The reason is firstly because many assign the highest probability of a catastrophic event happening to this kind of cause (apart perhaps from climate change) and because dealing with them raises very difficult questions of judgement. The prospect of super-intelligent AI having control of or access to significant resources is what most exercises people such as Ord or Bostrom. The simplest solution, which would indeed eliminate these risks were it to be adopted universally, is to simply not use any of these technologies. This 'Pavane' solution (after the science fiction novel of that name by Keith Roberts) would involve the prohibition of entire technologies (Roberts 2000). This kind of solution was suggested by Bostrom in his 2019 paper.

The first and obvious problem is that this would require an effective enforcement agency with global reach (the Catholic Church in the alternative history of Roberts), and nothing is currently available. However, we should be thankful for that, as the kind of global authority that Bostrom suggests would have near-totalitarian powers, not least with respect to research and investigation. This would be an example of the threat that worries his Oxford colleague Ord, a totalitarian authority. The other very serious difficulty is that even if we overlook the risks associated with the proposed institutions, this would mean forgoing enormous benefits, which are so significant that the loss (in the sense of forgoing them) would be close to the costs of something going catastrophically wrong (though not close if one thinks the risk existential). This means that fine judgements have to be made about the balance between risks and benefits and probabilities on both sides; on the one side, that of continuing to explore these technologies, are high probabilities of transformative benefits, as opposed to low probabilities of potentially infinite or at least catastrophic costs on the other.

This is a case where the two principles, the precautionary and the proactionary, have to be counterpoised. One reason for this is that many seriously pressing issues, including some other GCRs, will be much easier to address successfully if technologies such as AI are available (Winterson 2021). The outcome would be to continue research into these areas, not least because of the practical difficulty of making a total prohibition stick, while at the same time imposing strict controls or limits. A compromise position might be to pause certain types of research until a solution or defence against mishap has been developed. This has been proposed for AI, and a time-limited pause of this kind, as opposed to a total ban, makes a lot of sense. This is actually an example of a proactionary approach that if followed should make even time-limited bans rare. Risks need to be identified in new technologies and studied well before they arise and, should they prove to be actual as opposed to theoretical risks, we need to preemptively develop responses to them. In the case of AI, this is already underway, but there is still a long way to go. The point there is to think much more deeply and systematically about what the purpose of developing this technology is, and to think much more carefully about its architecture and control. One response would be to develop different kinds of AI as well as developing other technologies (including enhanced human capacity) that would make such developments less risky.

Widespread systems collapse

The challenge of a global systems collapse, of the kind that Letwin describes, is different to the others on this list in terms of what is required to prevent it. As regards the levels or types of action, this is a case where either the threat is headed off completely or only lifeboat measures remain. The challenge here is that if this is not solved, then eventually a major systems failure is very likely, the only question remaining is whether it will be global, or (more likely) regional but affecting a large part of the planet. The good news is that the measures to be taken are clear and obvious. The bad news is that they will be difficult without institutional reform, with those reforms facing collective action problems.

The solution is to simply change the way systems of all kinds, in business, government, finance and everyday life, work. We need to make systems more resilient (with higher levels of redundancy and work-around), more robust and less prone to cascade failure and collapse, and more secure and less susceptible to attack and subversion. This is partly a matter of design but also one of often keeping several systems in existence in parallel (keeping a functioning landline telephone system alongside a mobile one, for example). It also means relying upon older, physical technologies and systems as well as digital – using paper records as well as digital or maintaining analogue- and physical-based payments systems as well as electronic.

This is a simple idea but difficult to achieve at present because measures of this kind can be seen as costly and inefficient. This ignores the reality that the losses from a single catastrophic systems failure would be several times larger than the savings from years of using a less resilient technology or system. However, it also reflects challenges that are relevant for several of the GCRs discussed here – the increasingly short time horizons and high-return demands of many contemporary investment markets.

This is partly a cultural matter, reflecting a move in the later twentieth century towards individualism, and the decline of institutions and social norms that embed decisions in a multi-generational perspective, but it also reflects the impact of the increasingly deranged monetary system, something that can be traced back to at least the 1990s, or even the 1970s. We need, therefore, the kinds of strategic change set out earlier, particularly the move to a greater focus on the long term with regard to investment, and reform of the world monetary system. This is possible, but for private actors there is a serious collective action problem: any individual firm, institution or sector that moves this way will lose out, and so nothing will happen unless there is certainty that the change will be universal. This means that governmental action of some kind is required, the challenge being to succeed in this while not choking off innovation.

Political GCRs: war, terrorism, tyranny

GCRs that arise from human ill-will or misjudgement are in one sense impossible to avert at source, given the inexhaustible supply of both of these. However, this is also an area where the solutions lie purely within the realm of politics rather than technology. With regard to a large-scale nuclear exchange, the ultimate solution has to be a prohibition on the production of such weapons, similar to the successful prohibition of biological weapons of mass destruction. This is actually more achievable than many realise because of the incentives involved.

Regarding arms control negotiations and agreements (which is what we speak of here), the parties do indeed face a prisoner's dilemma in which the dominant strategy is to defect. However, this is a case where the negative payoff of pursuing the dominant strategy can be so large and so apparent that it makes sense for all parties, however rivalrous, to find a way to cooperate and deter defectors. In this case, the dynamics of a multi-polar world with a limited number of great powers are actually more conducive to cooperation than a world in which there is only one great power, although not hegemonic, plus a number of lesser powers (the present situation). In this latter case, it is not in the interests of the lesser powers to agree to a ban on nuclear weapons, because that would consolidate the dominant position of the main power. In the first case (the emergent one), all of the great powers, however competitive, have self-interest in preventing proliferation and removing the existential threat of an accidental but civilisation-ending exchange.

Concerning terrorism, the GCRs arise out of what we might call nihilistic terrorism, aiming deliberately at the destruction of civilisation or even the extermination of the human species. This is clearly a case where all powers have an interest in preventing such a thing from happening, through cooperation. Moreover, despite popular fantasies, terrorist organisations require a patron state or haven to have any real chance of large-scale impact. It is not in the realistic national interests of any great power in a stable multi-state system to encourage and sustain such 'fourth generation warfare' actors beyond a very low level. This means the political risks of a terrorist GCR are low and preventable, as long as a form of realism guides the security policies of the major states. It is the absence of that which poses the main threat.

As far as the prospect of a long-lasting and pervasive tyranny is concerned, the technological risk of this is real and significant. Technologies that can promote and facilitate extensive surveillance and control can also, paradoxically, make such control easier to evade and cir-cumvent, whether it comes from official state or nominally private actors (Friedman 2011). More fundamentally, this is a political challenge rather than a technological one. The way to head off this risk is through social and political action, which would include everything from mainstream politics to cultural 'metapolitics' and, crucially, the crea-tion of countervailing institutions that would prevent such a tyranny from being able to establish or sustain itself. One benefit here is that this risk only becomes truly global if the tyranny in question has global reach; if parts of the world escape it, then it has not been realised, despite the costs.

8 CONCLUSION

In this work the first step was to define global catastrophic risks, an apparently simple matter but important because of the persistent tendency to label anything that is both large in its impact and very bad as being one. On analysis, it turns out that much placed into that category is either not severe enough to count as catastrophic or, while catastrophic in impact, would not affect the entire planet and human species. This leaves a more precisely defined and limited category. By their nature, such risks require a special way of thinking, including the way potential loss is calculated.

The next step was to survey the range of risks that fall into the defined GCR category – an apparently eclectic range of possible events, ranging from the obvious and topical (such as pandemics) to the seemingly fanciful and speculative (such as hostile and super-powerful AI). We revealed a number of varieties of GCR, depending on the nature of the immediate cause of such an event were it to occur. The central argument is a probabilistic one that in many cases the risks are real and should be taken seriously. This is because, even though the probability of most of these events happening is low, the results, should any of

them be realised, range from staggeringly large (for catastrophic risks) to infinite (for existential risks). This in turn
means that many of the ways of thinking about risk and
cost–benefit trade-offs are hard or impossible to apply.
The appropriate way to think about these scenarios is as
bets with a terminal outcome for civilisation as a whole.
This should have the effect of concentrating the mind and
bringing clarity.

We have not entered into as much detail as we could
have done with regard to what the responses should be, not
least because each case would require a book of its own.
What is more important is to apply economic reasoning to
this, which has been sadly lacking so far. What that tells us
is that the often-posited trade-off between worrying about
GCRs and addressing more pressing immediate problems
does not actually exist. It also tells us that there are certain
approaches we should take in dealing with GCRs. There is
undoubtedly a need for government action in some areas,
often of a decisive kind. However, we should not fall into
the trap of thinking that large government-led projects
or actions are the only way to proceed. In particular, we
should not think that in anything other than a few of these
cases the only effective response is a global government or
its equivalent, not least because this way of thinking leads
to despair and fatalism. For this, the counterintuitive conclusion is that, more than ever, we need dispersed, decentralised networks that bring together the innovations and
creative responses of millions of people.

LINKS

Bulletin of the Atomic Scientists (1945)
https://thebulletin.org

Long Now Foundation (1996)
https://longnow.org

Machine Intelligence Research Institute (2000)
https://intelligence.org

Millennium Alliance for Humanity and
the Biosphere (2000)
https://mahb.stanford.edu

Nuclear Threat Initiative (2001)
https://www.nti.org

Future of Humanity Institute (2005)
https://www.fhi.ox.ac.uk

Lifeboat Foundation (2009)
https://lifeboat.com

Global Catastrophic Risks Institute (2011)
https://gcrinstitute.org

Global Challenges Foundation (2012)
https://globalchallenges.org

Centre for the Study of Existential Risk (2012)
https://www.cser.ac.uk

Future of Life Institute (2014)
https://futureoflife.org

Center on Long-Term Risk (2016)
https://longtermrisk.org

Center for Security and Emerging Technology (2019)
http://cset.georgetown.edu

Centre for Long-Term Resilience (2021)
https://www.longtermresilience.org

Existential Risk Observatory (2021)
https://www.existentialriskobservatory.org

Cathedral Thinking
https://cathedralthinking.com

LongBets
https://longbets.org

SciCast
https://scicast.org

Metaculus
https://www.metaculus.com/questions/

Intelligence Advanced Research Activity
https://www.iarpa.gov

Good Judgment Project
https://goodjudgment.com

REFERENCES

Acemoglu, D. (2021) The right way to worry. *Project Syndicate*, 14 May (https://www.project-syndicate.org/onpoint/how-to-think-about-existential-and-immediate-risks-by-daron-acemoglu-2021-05).

Adapt Research (2019) Pandemic catastrophe: 'lifeboat' is the wrong metaphor (https://adaptresearchwriting.com/2019/10/04/pandemic-catastrophe-lifeboat-is-the-wrong-metaphor/).

Alley, R. B. (2000) *The Two-Mile Time Machine: Ice Cores, Abrupt Climate Change and Our Future*. Princeton University Press.

Alley, R. B. et al. (2003) Abrupt climate change. *Science* 299(5615): 2005–10.

Ambrose, S. H. (1998) Late Pleistocene human population bottlenecks, volcanic winter, and differentiation of modern humans. *Journal of Human Evolution* 34(6): 623–51.

Anderson, E. (1995) *Value in Ethics and Economics*. Cambridge, MA: Harvard University Press.

Angell, N. (2012 [1910]) *The Great Illusion: A Study of the Relation of Military Power to National Advantage*. San Francisco, CA: Bottom of the Hill Publishing.

Avin, S. et al. (2018) Classifying global catastrophic risks. *Futures* 102 (September): 20–26.

Bashan, A. et al. (2013) The extreme vulnerability of interdependent spatially embedded networks. *Nature Physics* 9(10): 667–72.

Baum, S. D. et al. (2019) Long-term trajectories of human civilisation. *Foresight* 21(1): 53–83.

Beck, M. and Kewell, B. (2014) *Risk: A Study of Its Origins, History and Politics*. London: World Scientific.

Beckerman, W. (1974) *In Defence of Economic Growth*. London: Jonathan Cape.

Beckerman, W. (1996) *Small Is Stupid: Blowing the Whistle on the Greens*. London: Gerald Duckworth and Co.

Beckstead, N. and Ord, T. (2014) Managing existential risk from emerging technologies. In *Annual Report of the Chief Scientific Advisor 2014. Innovation: Managing Risk, Not Avoiding It. Evidence and Case Studies*, ch. 10. London: Government Office for Science.

Bendell, J. (2023) *Breaking Together: A Freedom-Loving Response to Collapse*. Bristol: Good Works.

Benton, M. J. (2003) *When Life Nearly Died: The Greatest Mass Extinction of All Time*. London: Thames and Hudson.

Blainey, G. (1988 [1973]) *The Causes of War*, 3rd edn. London: Free Press.

Body, R. (1982) *Agriculture: The Triumph and the Shame*. London: Avebury.

Bostrom, N. (2002) Existential risks: analysing human extinction scenarios and related hazards. *Journal of Evolution and Technology* 9(1) (https://www.nickbostrom.com/existential/risks.html).

Bostrom, N. (2003) Are you living in a computer simulation? *Philosophical Quarterly* 53(211): 243–55.

Bostrom, N. (2016) *Superintelligence: Paths, Dangers, Strategies*. Oxford University Press.

Bostrom, N. (2019) The vulnerable world hypothesis. *Global Policy* 10(4): 455–76.

Bostrom, N. and Cirkovic, M. M. (eds) (2012 [2008]) *Global Catastrophic Risks*. Oxford University Press.

Bourne, R. (2021) *Economics in One Virus: An Introduction to Economic Reasoning Through Covid-19*. Washington, DC: Cato Institute.

Brannen, P. (2017) *The Ends of the World: Volcanic Apocalypses, Lethal Oceans, and Our Quest to Understand Earth's Past Mass Extinctions*. London: Harper Collins.

Brovkin, V. et al. (2021) Past abrupt changes, tipping points and cascading impacts in the Earth system. *Nature Geoscience* 14(8): 550–58.

Brown, H. (1954) *The Challenge of Man's Future*. New York: Viking.

Buchanan, J. M. and Tullock, G. (1999 [1962]) *The Calculus of Consent: Logical Foundations of Constitutional Democracy*. Indianapolis, IN: Liberty Fund.

Buldryev, S. V., Parshani, R., Paul, G., Stanley, H. E. and Havlin, S. (2010) Catastrophic cascade of failures in interdependent networks. *Nature* 464(7291): 1025–28.

Calder, N. (1974) *The Weather Machine and the Threat of Ice*. London: BBC.

Carlin, D. (2019) *The End Is Always Near: Humanity vs the Apocalypse, from the Bronze Age to Today*. London: Collins.

Carson, R. (1962) *Silent Spring*. New York: Houghton Mifflin.

Ceballos, G., Ehrlich, A. and Ehrlich, P. (2015) *The Annihilation of Nature: Human Extinction of Birds and Mammals*. Baltimore, MD: Johns Hopkins University Press.

Cheatham, B., Javanmardian, K. and Samandari, H. (2019) Confronting the risks of artificial intelligence. *McKinsey Quarterly*, 26 April (https://www.mckinsey.com/capabilities/quantumb lack/our-insights/confronting-the-risks-of-artificial-intellig ence).

Chivers, T. (2020) *The Rationalist's Guide to the Galaxy: Superintelligent AI and the Geeks Who Are Trying to Save Humanity's Future.* London: Weidenfeld and Nicolson.

Christopher, J. (2009 [1956]) *The Death of Grass.* London: Penguin Modern Classics.

Cirillo, P. and Taleb, N. N. (2016) What are the chances of war? *Significance* 13(2): 44–45 (https://www.fooledbyrandomness .com/longpeace.pdf).

Clark, C. (2012) *The Sleepwalkers: How Europe Went to War in 1914.* London: Penguin.

Cole, H. S. D. (1973) *Models of Doom: A Critique of the Limits to Growth.* London: Universe Publishing.

Cox, J. (2005) *Climate Crash: Abrupt Climate Change and What It Means for Our Future.* Washington, DC: Joseph Henry Press.

De Cecco, F. and Orlando, G. (2020) What is the probability that new epidemic phenomena could occur in future? A probabilistic big data analysis to prevent the emergence and spread of future epidemics. PQE Group Infodemic (https://www.pqe group.com/wp-content/uploads/2020/07/ENG-PQE-Group -Infodemic-Project-What-is-the-probability-that-new-epide mic-phenomena-could-occur-in-future.pdf).

De Grey, A. and Rae, M. (2016) *Ending Aging: The Rejuvenation Breakthroughs That Could Reverse Human Aging in Our Lifetime.* New York: St. Martins Griffin.

Drexler, E. (1988) *Engines of Creation: The Coming Era of Nanotechnology.* New York: Anchor Books.

Duke, A. (2018) *Thinking in Bets: Making Smarter Decisions When You Don't Have All the Facts.* London: Penguin.

Ehrlich, P. (1968) *The Population Bomb.* New York: Ballantine.

Ferguson, N. (2021) *Doom: The Politics of Catastrophe*. London: Allen Lane.

Fisher, R. (2019) The perils of short-termism: civilisation's greatest threat. BBC, 10 January (https://www.bbc.com/future/article/20220805-what-is-longtermism-and-why-does-it-matter).

Friedman, D. (2011) *Future Imperfect: Technology and Freedom in an Uncertain World*. Cambridge University Press.

Fuller, S. and Lipinska, V. (2014) *The Proactionary Imperative: A Foundation for Transhumanism*. London: Palgrave Macmillan.

Garrett, L. (2020 [1994]) *The Coming Plague: Newly Emerging Diseases in a World Out of Balance*. New York: Picador.

Gates, B. (2021) *How to Avoid a Climate Disaster: The Solutions We Have and the Breakthroughs We Need*. London: Penguin.

Greer, J. M. (2008) *The Long Descent: A User's Guide to the End of the Industrial Age.* Gabriola Island, Canada: New Society Publishers.

Haldane, J. B. S. (1924) *Daedalus: Or, Science and the Future*. London: E P Dutton.

Hall, C. A. S., Lambert, J. G. and Balogh, S. B. (2014) EROEI of different fuels and the implications for society. *Energy Policy* 64: 141–52.

Harvey, F. (2020) Humanity under threat from perfect storm of crises – study. *The Guardian*, 6 February (https://www.theguardian.com/environment/2020/feb/06/humanity-under-threat-perfect-storm-crises-study-environment).

Heinberg, R. (2006) *Fifty Million Farmers*. Great Barrington, MA: Schumacher Center for New Economics.

Heinlein, R. A. (2016 [1956]) *Time for the Stars*. Rockville, MD: Phoenix Pick.

Herwig, H. H. (2002) Germany and the 'short war' illusion: towards a new interpretation. *Journal of Military History* 66(3): 681–93.

Homer, A. (2018) Earth will be hit by an asteroid with 100% certainty, says space watching group B612. *Inquistr*, 28 April (http://web.archive.org/web/20180429031332/https://www.inquisitr.com/4881237/earth-will-be-hit-by-an-asteroid-with-100-percent-certainty-says-space-watching-group-b612/).

Howard, M. (1984) Men against fire: expectations of war in 1914. *International Security* 9(1): 41–57.

Huebner, J. (2005) A possible declining trend for worldwide innovation. *Technological Forecasting and Social Change* 72(8): 980–86.

Jefferies, J. R. (1885) *After London or Wild England*. London: Cassell.

Jensen, D. (2006) *Endgame*, vol. I: *The Problem of Civilisation*. New York: Seven Stories Press.

Johnson, W. A. (2010 [1980]) *Muddling Towards Frugality: A New Social Logic for a Sustainable World*. Westport, CT: Easton Studio Press.

Junger, E. (2004 [1920]) *Storm of Steel*. London: Penguin.

Kaczynski, T. (2020) *Industrial Society and Its Future: The Unabomber Manifesto*. Independently published.

Kelman, I. (2020) *Disaster by Choice: How Our Actions Turn Natural Hazards into Catastrophes*. Oxford University Press.

Keys, D. (2000) *Catastrophe: An Investigation into the Origins of the Modern World*. London: Arrow Books.

Koch, R. (2022) *The 80/20 Principle: Achieve More with Less*. London: Nicholas Brealey.

Kurzweill, R. (2006) *The Singularity Is Near: When Humans Transcend Biology*. London: Duckworth.

Lenton, T. M. et al. (2008) Inaugural article: tipping points in the Earth's climate system. *Proceedings of the National Academy of Sciences* 105(6): 1786–93.

Lenton, T. M. et al. (2019) Climate tipping points – too risky to bet against. *Nature* 575(7784): 592–95.

Letwin, O. (2020) *Apocalypse How?: Technology and the Threat of Disaster.* London: Atlantic Books.

Lieven, A. (2020) *Climate Change and the Nation State: The Case for Nationalism in a Warming World.* Oxford University Press.

Lipsitch, M. (2018) Why do exceptionally dangerous gain-of-function experiments in influenza? In *Influenza Virus: Methods and Protocols* (ed. Y. Yamauchi), pp. 589–608. Springer (https:// link.springer.com/protocol/10.1007/978-1-4939-8678-1_29).

Liu, C. (2016) *The Dark Forest.* London: Head of Zeus.

Lloyds and Atmospheric and Environmental Research Inc. (2013) Solar storm risk to the North American electric grid. Report. London: Lloyds.

Lovelock, J. (2004) Nuclear power is the only green solution. *The Independent*, 24 May (http://www.jameslovelock.org/nuclear -power-is-the-only-green-solution/).

MacAskill, W. (2015) *Doing Good Better: Effective Altruism and a Radical Way to Make a Difference.* London: Guardian Faber.

MacAskill, W. (2022) *What We Owe the Future: A Million Year View.* London: OneWorld Publications.

McGuinness, P. (ed.) (2003) *T. E. Hulme: Selected Writings.* London: Fyfield Books.

McGuire, B. (2002) *A Guide to the End of the World: Everything You Ever Wanted to Know.* Oxford University Press.

McGuire, B. (2005) *Raging Planet: Earthquakes, Volcanoes and the Tectonic Threat to Life on Earth.* London: Quarto.

McGuire, B. (2009) *Global Catastrophes: A Very Short Introduction*. Oxford University Press.

McMillen, C. (2016) *Pandemics: A Very Short Introduction*. Oxford University Press.

Mannheim, D. (2018) Questioning estimates of natural pandemic risk. *Health Security* 16(6): 381–90 (https://www.ncbi.nlm.nih.gov/pmc/articles/PMC6306648/).

Marani, M., Katul, G. K., Pan, W. K. and Parolari, A. J. (2021) Intensity and frequency of extreme novel pandemics. *Proceedings of the National Academy of Sciences of the United States of America* 118(35).

Mazzucato, M. (2021) *Mission Economy: A Moonshot Guide To Changing Capitalism*. London: Allen Lane.

Meadows, D. H., Meadows, D. L. and Randers, J. (1972) *The Limits to Growth*. New York: Universe Books.

Meadows, D. H., Meadows, D. L. and Randers, J. (1992) *Beyond the Limits*. Chelsea, Vermont: Chelsea Green Publishing.

Meadows, D. H. and Randers, J. (2004) *Limits to Growth: The Thirty Year Update*. Chelsea, Vermont: Chelsea Green Publishing.

Mithen, S. (2004) *After the Ice: A Global Human History, 20,000 to 5,000 BC*. London: WandN.

Monbiot, G. (2023) *Regenesis: Feeding the World without Devouring the Planet*. London: Penguin.

More, M. (2013) The proactionary principle: optimising technological outcomes. In *The Transhumanist Reader: Classical and Contemporary Essays on the Science, Technology, and Philosophy of the Human Future* (ed. M. More and N. Vita-More). London: Wiley.

Morgan, T. (2013) *Life after Growth: How the Global Economy Really Works – And Why Two Hundred Years of Growth Are Over*. London: Harriman House.

Morris, I. (2015) *War: What Is It Good For? The Role of Conflict in Civilisation, from Primates to Robots.* London: Profile Books.

Moynihan, T. (2020) *X-Risk: How Humanity Discovered Its Own Extinction.* Falmouth: Urbanomic Media.

Müller, V. C. and Bostrom, N. (2016) Future progress in artificial intelligence: a survey of expert opinion. In *Fundamental Issues of Artificial Intelligence* (ed. V. C. Müller), pp. 555–72. Berlin: Springer.

National Research Council (2002) *Abrupt Climate Change: Inevitable Surprises.* Washington, DC: The National Academies Press.

Ord, T. (2020) *The Precipice: Existential Risk and the Future of Humanity.* London: Bloomsbury Press.

Ord, T. (2021) Politicians need to pay attention to existential risks. *Wired Magazine*, 21 August (https://www.wired.co.uk/ article/existential-risk-catastrophe-future-proof).

Ord, T., Hillerbrand, R. and Sandberg, A. (2010) Probing the improbable: methodological challenges for risks with low probabilities and high stakes. *Journal of Risk Research* 13(2): 191–205.

Osborn, F. (1948) *Our Plundered Planet.* London: Faber and Faber.

Ostrom, E. (2012) *The Future of the Commons: Beyond Market Failure and Government Regulations.* London: Institute of Economic Affairs.

Ostrom, E. (2015 [1990]) *Governing the Commons: The Evolution of Institutions for Collective Action.* Cambridge University Press.

Ostrom, E. and Ostrom, V. (2014) *Choice, Rules, and Collective Action: The Ostroms on the Study of Institutions and Governance.* ECPR Press.

Parker, G. (2013) *Global Crisis: War, Climate Change, and Catastrophe in the Seventeenth Century.* New Haven, CT: Yale University Press.

Parker, G. and Smith, L. M. (eds) (1997) *The General Crisis of the Seventeenth Century.* London: Routledge.

Pearse, P. (2012) Peace and the Gael (1915). In *The Coming Revolution: The Political Writings and Speeches of Patrick Pearse.* Blackrock, Cork: Mercier Press.

Pennington, M. (2010) *Robust Political Economy: Classical Liberalism and the Future of Public Policy.* Cheltenham: Edward Elgar.

Pinker, S. (2012) *The Better Angels of Our Nature: A History of Violence and Humanity.* London: Penguin.

Posner, R. (2004) *Catastrophe: Risk and Response.* Oxford University Press.

Quammen, D. (2013) *Spillover: Animal Infections and the Next Human Pandemic.* New York: Vintage.

Ravilious, K. (2005) What a way to go. *The Guardian*, 14 April (https://www.theguardian.com/science/2005/apr/14/research.science2).

Rees, M. (2003) *Our Final Century: Will the Human Race Survive the Twenty-First Century?* London: Heinemann.

Ridley, M. (2020) *How Innovation Works.* London: Fourth Estate.

Ripple, W. J. et al. (2021) World scientists' warning of a climate emergency 2021. *Bioscience* 71: 894–98.

Roberts, K. (2000 [1968]) *Pavane.* London: Gateway.

Russell, B. (1924) *Icarus: Or, The Future of Science.* London: E. P. Dutton.

Sabin, P. (2013) *The Bet: Paul Ehrlich, Julian Simon, and Our Gamble over Earth's Future.* New Haven, CT: Yale University Press.

Schneier, B. (2015) Resources on existential risk. Future of Life Institute (https://futureoflife.org/data/documents/Existential%20Risk%20Resources%20(2015-08-24).pdf).

Servigne, P. and Stevens, R. (2020) *How Everything Can Collapse.* Medford, MA: Polity Press.

Shiel, M. P. (1929 [1901]) *The Purple Cloud.* London: Gollancz.

Smil, V. (2012) *Global Catastrophes and Trends: The Next Fifty Years.* Cambridge, MA: MIT Press.

Smil, V. (2017) *Energy and Civilisation: A History.* Cambridge, MA: MIT Press.

Smil, V. (2021) *Grand Transitions: How the Modern World Was Made.* Oxford University Press.

Sombart, W. (2021 [1915]) *Traders and Heroes: Patriotic Reflections.* Arktos Media.

Sornette, D. and Cauwels, P. (2014) A creepy world. SFI Research Paper 13-55. Zurich: Swiss Finance Institute (https://papers.ssrn.com/sol3/papers.cfm?abstract_id=2388739).

Strumsky, D., Lobo, J. and Tainter, J. (2010) Complexity and the productivity of innovation. *Systems Research and Behavioural Science* 27(5): 496–509 (https://onlinelibrary.wiley.com/doi/full/10.1002/sres.1057).

Sunstein, C. R. (2006) *Laws of Fear: Beyond the Precautionary Principle.* Cambridge University Press.

Sunstein, C. R. (2021) *Averting Catastrophe: Decision Theory for Covid-19, Climate Change, and Potential Disasters of All Kinds.* New York: NYU Press.

Surowiecki, J. (2005) *The Wisdom of Crowds: Why the Many Are Smarter Than the Few.* London: Abacus.

Tainter, J. (1990) *The Collapse of Complex Societies.* Cambridge University Press.

Taleb, N. N. (2017) The logic of risk-taking. *Incerto*, 25 August (https://medium.com/incerto/the-logic-of-risk-taking-107bf41029d3).

Taleb, N. N. (2018) *Skin in the Game: Hidden Asymmetries in Daily Life*. London: Penguin.

Taleb, N. N., Bar-Yam, Y. and Cirillo, P. (2020a) On single point forecasts for fat-tailed variables. *International Journal of Forecasting* (https://www.ncbi.nlm.nih.gov/pmc/articles/PMC75 72356/).

Taleb, N. N., Norman, J. and Bar-yam, Y. (2020b) Systemic risks of pandemic via novel pathogens – coronavirus: a note. New England Complex Systems Institute, 26 January (https://static1 .squarespace.com/static/5b68a4e4a2772c2a206180a1/t/5e2e faa2ff2cf27efbe8fc91/1580137123173/Systemic_Risk_of_Pan demic_via_Novel_Path.pdf).

Tallis, R. (1991) *The Explicit Animal: Defence of Human Consciousness*. London: Palgrave Macmillan.

Turchin, A. and Denkenberger, D. (2018) Global catastrophic and existential risks communication scale. *Futures* 102 (September): 27–38.

Turner, G. (2014) Is global collapse imminent? MSSI Research Paper no. 4. Melbourne Sustainable Society Institute, University of Melbourne.

Vacca, R. (1974) *The Coming Dark Age*. New York: Anchor.

Vogt, W. (1948) *Road to Survival*. New York: William Sloane.

Wadhams, P. (2016) *A Farewell to Ice: A Report from the Arctic*. London: Allen Lane.

Wagar, W. W. (1982) *Terminal Visions: Literature of Last Things*. London: Wiley.

Williams, R. (2021) Whose streets? Our streets! 2020–21 'Smart City' cautionary trends and 10 calls to action to protect and promote democracy. Report. Cambridge, MA: Belfer Center

for Science and International Affairs (https://www.belfer
center.org/sites/default/files/2021-08/WhoseStreets.pdf).

Winterson, J. (2021) *12 Bytes: How Artificial Intelligence Will
Change the Way We Live and Love*. London: Jonathan Cape.

ABOUT THE IEA

The Institute is a research and educational charity (No. CC 235 351), limited by guarantee. Its mission is to improve understanding of the fundamental institutions of a free society by analysing and expounding the role of markets in solving economic and social problems.

The IEA achieves its mission by:

- a high-quality publishing programme
- conferences, seminars, lectures and other events
- outreach to school and college students
- brokering media introductions and appearances

The IEA, which was established in 1955 by the late Sir Antony Fisher, is an educational charity, not a political organisation. It is independent of any political party or group and does not carry on activities intended to affect support for any political party or candidate in any election or referendum, or at any other time. It is financed by sales of publications, conference fees and voluntary donations.

In addition to its main series of publications, the IEA also publishes (jointly with the University of Buckingham), *Economic Affairs*.

The IEA is aided in its work by a distinguished international Academic Advisory Council and an eminent panel of Honorary Fellows. Together with other academics, they review prospective IEA publications, their comments being passed on anonymously to authors. All IEA papers are therefore subject to the same rigorous independent refereeing process as used by leading academic journals.

IEA publications enjoy widespread classroom use and course adoptions in schools and universities. They are also sold throughout the world and often translated/reprinted.

Since 1974 the IEA has helped to create a worldwide network of 100 similar institutions in over 70 countries. They are all independent but share the IEA's mission.

Views expressed in the IEA's publications are those of the authors, not those of the Institute (which has no corporate view), its Managing Trustees, Academic Advisory Council members or senior staff.

Members of the Institute's Academic Advisory Council, Honorary Fellows, Trustees and Staff are listed on the following page.

The Institute gratefully acknowledges financial support for its publications programme and other work from a generous benefaction by the late Professor Ronald Coase.

Other books recently published by the IEA include:

Ayn Rand: An Introduction
Eamonn Butler
ISBN 978-0-255-36764-6; £12.50

Capitalism: An Introduction
Eamonn Butler
ISBN 978-0-255-36758-5; £12.50

Opting Out: Conscience and Cooperation in a Pluralistic Society
David S. Oderberg
ISBN 978-0-255-36761-5; £12.50

Getting the Measure of Money: A Critical Assessment of UK Monetary Indicators
Anthony J. Evans
ISBN 978-0-255-36767-7; £12.50

Socialism: The Failed Idea That Never Dies
Kristian Niemietz
ISBN 978-0-255-36770-7; £17.50

Top Dogs and Fat Cats: The Debate on High Pay
Edited by J. R. Shackleton
ISBN 978-0-255-36773-8; £15.00

School Choice around the World … And the Lessons We Can Learn
Edited by Pauline Dixon and Steve Humble
ISBN 978-0-255-36779-0; £15.00

School of Thought: 101 Great Liberal Thinkers
Eamonn Butler
ISBN 978-0-255-36776-9; £12.50

Raising the Roof: How to Solve the United Kingdom's Housing Crisis
Edited by Jacob Rees-Mogg and Radomir Tylecote
ISBN 978-0-255-36782-0; £12.50

How Many Light Bulbs Does It Take to Change the World?
Matt Ridley and Stephen Davies
ISBN 978-0-255-36785-1; £10.00

The Henry Fords of Healthcare … Lessons the West Can Learn from the East
Nima Sanandaji
ISBN 978-0-255-36788-2; £10.00

An Introduction to Entrepreneurship
Eamonn Butler
ISBN 978-0-255-36794-3; £12.50

Other IEA publications

Comprehensive information on other publications and the wider work of the IEA can be found at www.iea.org.uk. To order any publication please see below.

Personal customers

Orders from personal customers should be directed to the IEA:

IEA
2 Lord North Street
FREEPOST LON10168
London SW1P 3YZ
Tel: 020 7799 8911, Fax: 020 7799 2137
Email: sales@iea.org.uk

Trade customers

All orders from the book trade should be directed to the IEA's distributor:

Ingram Publisher Services UK
1 Deltic Avenue
Rooksley
Milton Keynes MK13 8LD
Tel: 01752 202301, Fax: 01752 202333
Email: ipsuk.orders@ingramcontent.com

IEA subscriptions

The IEA also offers a subscription service to its publications. For a single annual payment (currently £42.00 in the UK), subscribers receive every monograph the IEA publishes. For more information please contact:

Subscriptions
IEA
2 Lord North Street
FREEPOST LON10168
London SW1P 3YZ
Tel: 020 7799 8911, Fax: 020 7799 2137
Email: accounts@iea.org.uk